BEGINNERS LUCK GUIDE FOR NON-RUNNERS

Learn To Run From Scratch To An Hour In 10 Weeks

By George Anderson

www.ByGeorgeAnderson.com

1st Edition Published (Kindle Only) June 2013
2nd Edition Published July 2014
Kinetic Books

About the author

George Anderson is a running coach, writer, presenter and program creator. He has helped thousands of runners through his website www.runningbygeorge.com, and various training and nutrition programs.

As well as working with runners, George runs a group fitness and nutrition program in Oxfordshire called the Boot Camp.

George lives in Thame, Oxfordshire with his wife Laura and three children, Fern, Rowan and Gabriel. He finds running to be the perfect way to get some peace and quiet.

Contact George through social media:

facebook.com/coachgeorgeanderson
facebook.com/intelligentrunning
twitter.com/byGeorgeA
youtube.com/intelligentrunning

Or email george@bygeorgeanderson.com

Contents

Author's Notes   p4

Foreword   p6

Preface   p8

1. What are the first things I need to do to get started?   p10

2. How do I build up to running for 60 minutes?   p25

3. What kit do I really need?   p37

4. How do I stay motivated to run?   p49

5. What is the best way to warm up and cool down?   p51

6. How do I avoid getting injured?   p70

7. What should I eat to fuel my running?   p81

8. How can I improve the way I run?   p92

9. How do I run faster?   p100

10. How do I prepare for my first race?   p107

11. Frequently Asked Questions   p114

12. Final words   p118

13. The program   p119

Resources   p131

Author's Notes

Learning to run from scratch can be a daunting prospect, and possibly something that you've tried in the past without success. When I was writing this book I wanted to step inside the heads of as many beginner runners as possible so I set up a Facebook group to test out the program.

This online community proved to be exceptionally popular and I learned a great deal about the major challenges faced by non-runners, just like you, when starting out. The results of those lessons are contained within the pages of this book but, in an effort to give you all the help and support you need to make it stick, I have done two things.

Firstly, if you use Facebook you can join the group and chat to others who have gone through the exact same process. This support was invaluable for many of the beginners who helped me test out the program. Secondly, I have asked some of the beginner runners who were a part of the creation of this book to write a few words about their experiences to share with you.

Many of these messages are peppered throughout the book, and you'll find more of them, along with the lessons that were learned, over at the companion website: www.beginnersluckbook.com. On this website there is also a special invite to join the Facebook group where you can interact with other beginners, as well as those who have passed through the program.

*****

Thank you for purchasing the *Beginner's Luck Guide For Non-Runners.* I would really appreciate you taking a moment to leave me some feedback on Amazon, telling me what you thought. Your feedback is important to me because it inspires other beginners to take the same leap of faith that you just have, and will help me improve the next version of the book. Thank you so much!

Dedicated to my Dad, the original running inspiration

Foreword

I can still recall my first 'run'. If I am to be honest, I wasn't thinking about leopards or lions (this reference will make sense as you read Georges book). My primary motivation was to get home for a cigarette. Thankfully, 18 years later, I have long since dropped the smoking habit but I have never dropped the running. It has given me so much more than just physical exercise benefits. It has helped me in every aspect of my life. Of that I am certain.

It is an honour to offer a few words at the beginning of George's book. He and I first connected in 2011 and I have watched in admiration his enthusiasm for his clients to succeed and his passion for sharing simple yet vitally important knowledge on the art of running.

That is exactly what this book offers. Simple but brilliant tips covering the 'need to know' aspects that many books cover only in passing, as well as a thoroughly thought out, practical, accountable and elevating training plan that will challenge you but in a measured way.

This book has reminded me and reinforces a multitude of learning's that I myself have found over the years. I have enjoyed every page and I am confident you will too.

Gerry Duffy

Ultra Running Enthusiast
September 1 2013
Mullingar, Ireland

Beginner's Luck

Preface

I've been running since I was about 8 years old so can't ever remember a time when I would have considered myself a true beginner. Most of my programs and writing in the past have been aimed at people who were already running to varying degrees of success. Then, in September 2012 I was in Portugal at a coaching mastermind event and somebody said something, almost in passing, that was a real 'ah ha' moment.

"Every coach should have something to offer beginners", were the words that had such an impact on me. I realised that whilst I was already merrily helping several thousands of runners with the work I was doing over at RunningByGeorge.com, there were many thousands more on whose ears my work would never land.

I had worked with beginner runners in the past as a personal trainer and coach, but I certainly didn't have anything in the way of a comprehensive guide to offer. I soon became obsessed with solving this shortfall.

Having never written a book before, I had built it up in my mind as being an enormous task that would take an age to complete, assuming I did ever get started. Consequently, I deliberated and procrastinated, putting off starting the job until January 2013.

Over the course of the next 5 months, I obsessed over providing solutions to even the seemingly tiny challenges that beginner runners commonly face. The Facebook group was a goldmine of honest feedback on the program which forms the foundation of this book, and gave me an insight into the minds of dozens of beginner runners.

Without this ongoing feedback I am sure that I would have produced something completely different, based instead on my perception of what was required rather than the reality of beginner runners.

So, to all those men and women who joined me on this journey of *Beginner's Luck*, I thank you, not only personally, but also on behalf of everybody who benefits from the information contained within this book.

Chapter 1 – What are the first things I need to do to get started?

You've decided you're going to learn how to run and are sitting there feeling all motivated and perhaps slightly scared about the challenge that lies ahead but... what happens next?

Or rather, what happens first? All the information you need to get cracking is in this book, but in this chapter I want to lay down the first steps you should take, the considerations you should make, and the foundations you should lay down in order to make this a success. After all, this isn't really about just starting to run, this is about creating a habit of running in such a way that you actually enjoy it and want to get out there for more.

If you've been burnt by running in the past, you may already have a negative mind-set about how hard it's going to be. But my aim is to change all that and show you that anybody, including *you*, can learn how to run for an hour and beyond.

First things first

One thing I've learned that works over and over again is to set your desired outcomes and expectations right at the start. Not just in physical challenges like this one, but in anything that you do.

In this case, have a careful think about what it is you hope to achieve with the program, why that is important to you, and how you will be able to identify when you have been successful.

Of course, you could just skip this step and head out for Bobcat Week run one, but your chances of success would be greatly diminished. You most likely already have the answers to these questions inside your head, but you just need to put them into some kind of logical sequence and perhaps get them down onto a piece of paper.

If you're doing *Beginner's Luck* for weight loss, consider the possibility that running by itself won't be enough and that you may have to reassess your nutrition. You can't out-train a bad diet and I've seen many beginners quit in the past because it 'wasn't working'.

Perhaps you just want to 'feel a bit fitter'. Another excellent goal; I mean who *doesn't* want to feel a bit fitter? But how will you know when you have got there? How much fitter do you want to be and why is this level important to you?

Often beginners take up running because it presents a real but achievable challenge, especially when the end goal is some kind of race. But is this enough to keep you interested for 10 or more weeks? Have you considered what will happen when your challenge has been and gone? How will you feel when you are successful and what would the consequences be if things weren't to go your way?

Considering these thoughts right from the outset will set you up with a clear path and a simple method of assessing whether or not you are achieving what you want to.

When to quit

It's also worth pointing out that there's no shame in quitting; in fact it can often be the smart thing to do. This seems like a strange thing to say in the opening chapter of a book on how to run, but if you start running because you think it's going to give you something back, and then you hate every darned minute of it, pick another challenge!

If you follow *Beginner's Luck* to the letter you are far more likely to find the beginner's utopia of actually enjoying the process. However, if you give it your best shot but you still don't enjoy it then be prepared to say when enough is enough.

I quit stuff all the time, but only if I'm clearly not going to achieve my intended outcome. That's not to say I give up at the first challenge or obstacle. I persevere and understand that I may have to try things a myriad ways before I find the solution but I'm always prepared to quit if the pain of pursuing what I thought was important outweighs the potential benefits of achieving it.

Hopefully this won't be one of those outcomes for you but I wanted to throw it into the mix right from the outset.

Take away the pressure

Many beginners fail before they start because they pile far too much pressure on themselves. Some of that is down to the program they choose to follow, especially where it requires a set pace of progress each week. If you don't keep up, you fall behind schedule adding a great deal of unnecessary pressure. Sometimes, though, the pressure felt is self-imposed.

You'll read about how the Golden Key will change everything for you, unlocking your potential to run for longer and finding it easier than you ever thought would be possible. When you learn about this and apply it to your first run it's like undoing the valve on a pressure cooker. All of a sudden you realise that as long as you remember the Golden Key you can go on for much longer than you imagined and you begin to enjoy it more.

After all, enjoyment really should be one of the underlying motivations for doing this program. Even if you experience an element of discomfort at the time of doing it, running can be a truly joyful experience and it's worth keeping sight of this if you ever feel the pressure start to build.

Your rate of progress can also be a source of pressure. You'll discover when you read the program itself that thanks to the 10 Cats you don't have to stick to any kind of time schedule when you follow *Beginner's Luck*. You progress at your own rate which means if you can't get out for a few days or you find one run particularly challenging, you just extend the length of the Cat Week until you are confident you can move on.

This does wonders for relieving the pressure of being a beginner runner.

The Golden Key

I've heard lots of beginner runners say things like, "I just can't run", or, "I can barely run for a bus". You may even have said something similar yourself in the past. Well, what I have discovered is simple yet so unbelievably powerful that once you apply it to your running you'll notice an attitude-changing difference immediately.

What I saw happening with nearly all beginner runners was a tendency to start off way too fast. Think about the second of those common phrases for a moment: "I can barely run for a bus". If you had to run for a bus I'll bet you'd be running because it's about to leave and you want to be on it, so you have to run as fast as you possibly can!

"Without the Golden Key, I would have probably crashed and bailed out in the early days. I never thought about slowing down on my previous attempts of running and always thought it was about distance rather than time. Slowing down and running for a certain amount of time and not worrying about the distance made it so much more achievable."
– Amanda Bradfield

"The Golden Key put me at ease because I am a slow runner anyway; knowing I didn't have to go fast took away all the pressure."
– Yvonne Radley

"The Golden Key makes a huge difference as you realise it's not about the distance you cover, it's more about slowing it down and running for longer amounts of time. Whenever I'm running now and start to feel tired I literally take it back to basics."
– Debbie Maher

"Although there is a 10 week plan, it is just a guide and provides a good structure for a beginner like me. Thanks to some basic fitness, I started with 5 minutes slow jog intervals. Thanks to the "Golden Key" I managed it easily and amazed myself. It has taken longer than 10 weeks, due to other commitments, but yesterday I completed 60 minutes non-stop jogging! If you'd have told me that in Feb this year I would never have believed it"
- Jenni

But that's not the way we want to learn how to run on this program. *Beginner's Luck* is all about building up your running so you can confidently run for up to an hour and beyond. Nothing at all about how far you run. The Golden Key is to slow your pace down as much as you possibly can. Even if this means jogging at marginally faster than walking pace, you will suddenly find that you are able to go for much longer than you would if you were running at full pelt.

Even experienced runners struggle with this concept. If you ever watch a race you'll see hundreds of runners sprinting off at the start and then nearly collapsing just a few kilometers down the road. Running faster is harder than running slower, and although you may be able to hold that pace for a little while when you're fresh, it soon takes its toll.

Beginner's Luck isn't about distance. We'll talk about running faster and further in Chapter 9 but first things first: get confident with running continuously for longer periods of time.

A good friend of mine and highly experienced ultra-runner Warren Pole runs some of his races at 5km/h. That's slightly more than walking pace, but it's a pace that he's able to keep going for 24 hours or more as he competes in 100+ mile foot races. You may not go on to run ultra-marathons, but don't think for a second that the fact you're running slowly makes you any less of a runner.

I can't stress enough how important it is that you take the Golden Key with you on every run. Slow down, and I promise you will find that you can build up your running far easier than you ever imagined possible and you'll be shaking your head in disbelief at what you've just achieved. I recorded a video explaining the Golden Key and how critical it is for your success here: www.runningbygeorge.com/beginners/goldenkey

Where are you going to go?

The next thing to decide is where on earth are you going to run? You have two general options here: you can either run outdoors in the big wide world, or you can run on a treadmill. Although I'd encourage you to run outside whenever you have the opportunity, treadmills can be useful as you build up your confidence. Just bear in mind that it feels very different to running outside and you may find that a lot of treadmill running makes it harder when you eventually do venture out onto the streets.

"I started on a treadmill and found it great to build up my running confidence. Got some shock when I transitioned to outdoors – takes much more out of you but gives so much more back! I rarely visit the treadmill now."
– Karen Hill

One little tip I will give you for the treadmill, however, is to set the incline to 1% as this is just enough to give you a bit of vertical force and compensates the fact that you have no wind resistance on a running machine.

If you're going to take to the great outdoors to hone your skills as a runner, there are three main options for doing this: circuitous route, out and back, or out *or* back.

Circuitous route

I love that word don't you? It's got a lovely dancing rhythm to it like mellifluous or gymkhana. Sorry, I digress.

A circuitous route is where you start at a point, run a route, and end up back where you started from. It's perhaps the most common way of running, but it does rather depend on you knowing the area you're running in from a pedestrian's perspective, and also being able to estimate how far you're going to need to go for each run.

A good starting point would be to plot out a route of a half to a full mile and then run one or more loops for your first week of running. That will give you a feel for the distance you will cover for a given duration of running and you can then build up longer loops from there.

"I didn't like to stick to one route so I varied mine every time. The emphasis was on time and not distance so this helped me clear my mind and just enjoy the experience."
– Yvonne Radley

"I found running around the local sports field too boring, so started going on paths and tracks. I've been surprised how far I can run in 25-30 mins. More than I would have expected compared to walking."
– Mary-Jane Sharratt

Out and back

A lot of people don't like these types of runs because they think they're boring but I like the symmetry and also they are perfect for beginners. Say your session calls for 24 minutes overall, plus a 5 minute walk warm-up and cool-down. That's 34 minutes overall so for an out and back run you just head off in any direction that takes your fancy, do exactly half of the session (17 minutes in this case), and then turn around and head back again.

You may not finish on the exact same spot you started from but you won't be far off, making it much easier to plan.

Out OR back

Hardly anybody does the out *or* back style of route planning but I think it adds a nice element of adventure that may or may not appeal to you.

To make this work you need to have a good grasp of your local public transport services, or someone you can call to pick you up or drop you off. For the out or back run you would either run out for the entire duration of the session and then get a lift back home again, or get a lift out to a set point and make your way back on foot.

This does take a little more planning and probably isn't the best strategy for those first tentative footsteps of *Beginner's Luck*, but you may want to consider it for when your confidence is starting to brim a little more.

Training diary

This is as good a time as any to introduce the idea of a training diary, or training journal. Buy yourself a nice notebook and in it write the details of all the runs you do. For me, the devil is in the detail so I log things like distance, route, weather conditions, time taken, and maybe even the kit I wore. If you're more creative you may want to record your achievements more as a journal, telling the story of each run, things you saw and feelings you experienced along the way.

At the very least I'd recommend printing out the program from www.beginnersluckbook.com and sticking it on your fridge so you can tick off the runs as you do them. Some beginners have told me they found sticking gold stars by each of the runs as they are successfully completed enormously motivating!

However you record your training, it will serve as a bank of evidence that you are capable of doing this, if ever those dark, negative thoughts start setting in.

Good old-fashioned writing down is great, but there are also plenty of websites out there that allow you record all of this information online. I have listed a few in the Resources section at the back of this book but have a look around and find one that jumps out at you.

Book an appointment with yourself

The next consideration you need to make is when you are going to do this. It'll probably be in the morning before work, in a lunch break, during the day if you don't work, or after work in the evening.

Whenever you are planning on running, it's important to make an appointment with yourself.

When was the last time you missed a dentist appointment? Or an important meeting at work? Or what about missing a lunch date with an old friend you haven't seen in ages?

You make these appointments because they are in the diary and are important to you. Treat your running the same way otherwise it simply won't happen. If you run a diary, put your training in there and block out enough time to accommodate changing and showering.

Even better, find somebody else to run with and book a time to meet them. Much harder to talk yourself out of a run when somebody else is relying on you to be there for company.

What are you going to wear?

Chapter 3 is dedicated to kit, but for now you really don't have to worry about having any special gear. A comfy pair of trainers, top and bottoms that you feel comfortable exercising in and maybe one or two extra layers if it's cold or wet.

As I explain in the kit chapter, there's a whole heap of kit you can spend your money on when you get into running but not having lots of Lycra running gear shouldn't be a barrier to getting started. The most important thing to begin with is that you feel comfortable and warm.

Set yourself some process goals

We spoke earlier about your intended outcomes and expectations, which in some respects could be taken to be your big picture goals. Drop this down a level and you get your performance goals which include things like 'Be able to run for 20 minutes by the 1st of May' or 'Lose 5lb in the next 2 weeks'.

Go steady with setting these types of goals early on because they can pile on unnecessary pressure. You don't know what kind of progress you're going to make in the first few weeks so start off with just concentrating on moving from Cat to Cat within the program.

The third type of goal which you absolutely should set is a process goal. These goals are great because they are instantly achievable and completely within your control. They are things like 'Run three times this week' or 'Eat two more portions of vegetables every day this week' or even 'Spend five minutes stretching at the end of each run'.

As long as you have thought these goals through there should be nothing stopping you from achieving them. There's something very satisfying about being able to tick goals off a list very early on. They are a part of the process so if you do those things, you will achieve the performance goals and ultimately the big picture stuff like your intended outcome, so expectations will take care of themselves.

Some practical issues

If you're running from home you most likely have shower facilities waiting for you when you get back. Do you have the same facilities if you are running from work in a lunch break? How about carrying stuff with you on a run like your house or car key and mobile phone?

Most 'proper' running bottoms will have a little zip pocket where you can stash a key but if you are carrying a mobile phone you may want to run with a waist pack. I use these on my longer runs and when I'm racing marathons because they're lightweight, sit snuggly against my body and don't bounce up and down.

They also fit a mobile phone which is sensible to carry if you're unsure of exactly where you're going or feel you may need to call for back up at some point. Incidentally, any kit I mention specifically in this book is detailed in the Resources section at the end.

Water

On runs lasting less than an hour you don't really need to carry water with you. The level of dehydration you'll experience in this timeframe will not be enough to affect the way you feel; though if it's a particularly warm day you might want to consider taking a small bottle with you.

Forget about sports drinks: they're a marketing strategy on the most part and water really is your best bet especially on these less-than-the-hour sessions. There are bottles designed specifically for runners that are more conveniently-shaped to carry, or that fit into a little neoprene belt pack. I have listed links to a couple of my favourites in the Resources section at the back of this book. Another option would be to loop your run past your house a couple of times and place a bottle of water in the bushes so you can have a quick stop for a water break if you need it.

What will it feel like?

If you are stepping into the unknown, the stage before your first run can be particularly nerve-wracking. It's a big adventure and the uncertainty can be hard to bear. At some point you just have to get out there and crack on, but it's good to have an idea of what it might feel like along the way.

"Before my first run I felt a bit anxious about how I had been fooling myself that I could run again anytime I wanted. The program was just the ticket."
– Helen Conway

"I kept putting my first run off, and off, and off again. I thought it was gonna be easy. Jog 1 min, walk 2 mins – anyone can do that right? Err no! The stitch hit and the breathing was gasping, until I watched the video on how to breathe properly."
– Amanda Bradfield

I just didn't think I could do it, running didn't seem for me. I also didn't think I had ever seen a runner or jogger smiling as I went past them so wasn't sure of the 'fun factor' and I was always so self conscious when exercising. I also had

memories of terrible cross country runs at school where I always started with such enthusiasm and very quickly ended up at the back with the smokers!
- Anne-Marie Chapman

Self-consciousness

A lot of beginners report that they feel self-conscious when they start running. Almost like they shouldn't be doing it, like somehow they don't belong. If you're carrying some extra weight and running is a way to help you to lose it this can add to the self-conscious feelings.

A great way around this is to either run in the evening when the light is dimmer, or get out into the countryside where there are fewer people. In reality nobody will be looking at you and thinking anything other than, "Oh, there's a runner". If somebody sees you when you're in a walking interval it probably won't even compute that you're on this crazy adventure. In any case, *you're* the one out there doing something whilst most other people are sat at home on their couches doing nothing.

Running as slowly as I recommend you do can also make some people feel self-conscious, especially when passing 'real' runners. As somebody who has been running since he was 8, I can tell you that the vast majority of experienced runners have nothing but admiration for anybody who gets out there and does it. The moment you step out of your front door and 'go for a run' you become a part of a very welcoming community. And besides, if anybody is nosey enough to ask you why you're running so slowly just look them in the eye and tell them you're training for an ultra marathon.

How will it feel?

Everybody's experiences are different but there are a few physical changes you are bound to notice take place in your body. You're likely to find that your breathing and heart rate go up. You may even get a bit out of breath but this is fine; just remember the Golden Key and try to focus on the breathing pattern you'll learn about in Chapter 8 which is all about technique.

Your legs will start to ache. Most likely the thighs and possibly the lower legs. You'll start to sweat and probably begin to wish you'd left the jacket at home! Your face may go a kind of beetroot red colour (it won't actually, but that's what it'll feel like) and you'll probably be sore for a day or two after your first few runs.

But what a sense of achievement! How amazing will you feel when you come back in your front door having completed your first run, immediately sitting down at your computer or notebook to log your feelings and progress whilst it's still fresh in your mind? The smile from ear to ear that just won't go away as the 'runner's high' engulfs your body and your systems are flooded with endorphins.

The physical symptoms are indications that you are stressing your body so that it adapts and you become a better runner. The emotions and psychological symptoms are there to keep you motivated and engaged in the process, not just the goal of getting to the end of week 10.

Chapter 2 – How do I build up to running for 60 minutes?

If you've never run before the idea of running continuously for a whole hour may seem a little ambitious, and possibly a bit scary as well. You may have tried in the past, and struggled, to get beyond a certain point, so there may be an element of doubt in there too. Building up to running for 60 minutes from scratch is going to take time, perseverance and commitment, but it CAN be done.

Build up gradually

One of most important ingredients in the *Beginner's Luck* program is to build up your running gradually. It's a really common mistake to try and do too much too soon as I'll explain later, so the first thing we need to do is remove the Big Pressure:

Time.

I know, I know, time-framed, 'SMART' goals are great to have but when it comes to this type of running they can be the kiss of death.

As soon as you set yourself a goal like "I will run continuously for one hour by XYZ date" you pile on the Big Pressure. The thing is, you don't *know* how you're going to progress through the program and neither do I, so setting a time frame just doesn't make any sense.

Remember what your *real* goal is here: to gain confidence in your ability to run and to build running into your life. Running an hour just happens to be a nice round number

25

that most people can relate to, but hey, you get to 45, 30, or even 20 minutes and you're going to be feeling pretty pleased with yourself.

This program is about the journey: the transition from non-runner to confident runner and I have set it up in a way that will allow you to do exactly this.

Cat Levels

You'll notice from the program (see Chapter 12) that each week has a different cat name. This isn't just some quirky 'let's make this program a bit different' strategy, it has an important purpose. Each Level of training can last as long as you need it to last. There are three runs to complete each Level, but you don't move on to the next Level until you have successfully completed all the runs in the one you are on.

Let's assume you start Bobcat Week (the start of the program) on a Monday. You run Monday, Wednesday and Saturday but find the Saturday session difficult. You have to increase the amount of rest you take but you still get through to the end.

_____

"I like the cat theme – if it went up in numbers I would feel a mounting pressure to go higher and higher but take the numbers away and there's no pressure. Plus cats are empowering especially as you get to Cheetah and Cougar weeks, it makes you feel fearless."
– Yvonne Radley

"I loved working my way up and getting stronger week by week, especially liked transforming to a cougar. I kept a copy of the program on my fridge and ticked them off as

each one was completed: it was encouraging to see them falling off one by one."
– Amanda Bradfield

———————————

The following Monday, instead of moving onto week two of the program (as you may have done in the past regardless of how you were getting on) you just repeat the third session from Bobcat Week. This time you nail it and find you can do the whole session with the recoveries outlined in the program (I'll explain what's just happened here physically later in this chapter).

Only *now,* after another day of rest, are you ready to move on and so you hit your first run of Lynx Week on Wednesday.

Your next Level can start any day: you progress at YOUR pace when YOU are ready.

Q: "But doesn't having to repeat a session mean you're not making progress?"

A: "No."

Progress doesn't just have to be measured by the session you are up to in the program. By allowing yourself to repeat a session two, three or more times you can make smaller, incremental progressions without pushing yourself too hard (remember the number one reason new runners quit: too much too soon).

———————————

"The greatest thing is that although I can't consistently do great distances, every time I run (or jog in my case) I am able to increase the distance each time with relative comfort! This is a GREAT confidence booster. I actually feel fit for the first time in my life. In fact I even felt exhilarated the other

day after a 3.2 mile run (wow that feels amazing to be typing that!!)."
– Sarah Allen

If, say, you've done a run but had to extend the last couple of recovery times by 30 seconds, then the next time you attempt it you don't need those extra seconds... that's progression!

Move on to the next session ONLY when you are ready. The ten Level program may well only take you ten weeks to get through, but who cares if it takes you longer? Some beginners never make it to the full hour purely through choice. Being able to run for 45 minutes is all they ever wanted to achieve so why push beyond?

However long it takes, you will be making consistent progress throughout and you'll be a runner well before you get to the end.

Get FITTA

FITTA is one of those annoying acronyms that spells what it's describing. It stands for Frequency, Intensity, Time, Type, Adherence. They are all variables we can use to make sure we're progressing and becoming better, more confident runners. Let's quickly go through them so you can better understand the program.

Frequency

The most you should be running on this program is every other day. Your body needs a complete day of rest between every dose of running and even though sometimes you may feel fine the next day, it's important that you give yourself this complete break.

When you do a little bit more than your body is used to, you give it a bit of a shock. The systems in your body (like your muscles, nerves, heart and lungs) have to work harder and this causes a tiny amount of damage to occur.

This kind of damage is nothing to worry about; in fact it's good. The 'training effect' as it is called then causes a chain reaction of repair and growth as your body adapts to the stimulus, so when you next go out you're a little bit stronger.

BUT...

This can only happen if you give yourself enough time to recover. The whole process of training stimulus, shock, adaptation, repair and growth takes up to 48 hours. If you regularly reduce this recovery time you won't get all the lovely benefits from all of your hard work.

You can still do other exercise in between running sessions (like gym work, aerobics or other classes, or swimming) but lay off the running. At least one day a week you should take a complete break from structured exercise and allow your body to properly recover. This will not only help you progress faster, it will also reduce your chances of injury as your body becomes stronger.

It's very tempting in the early weeks to do more than 3 runs a week, but more often than not this stores up trouble for later on down the road. You may feel *capable* of running on back to back days, but that doesn't necessarily mean it's the best thing for you. The all or nothing approach rarely works when applied to Beginner's Luck.

Intensity

All the runs in the program should be taken at a low intensity. The faster you run, the higher the intensity of the training session. Sometimes this is a good thing but at the moment your mission is to get running for longer periods of time. Remember the Golden Key.

Time

Don't worry about speed or distance – it's all about the time right now. Your time (or training volume) can be measured in two ways: the number of running minutes accumulated and the total length of the session.

This builds up as the Levels progress, and although some sessions seem shorter than previous ones they will accumulate more minutes of running, or have shorter recovery periods between them. In the program in Chapter 12 it details the number of running minutes and the total duration of the session so you can see how it progresses each week.

Type

We're only interested in running here, but you may decide to combine this program with other exercise such as aerobics classes, swimming, boot camp-style workouts or gym work.

Getting a variety of different types of exercise is good but, let's face it, you want to learn to run so this should be your priority.

Adherence

My favourite one! It doesn't matter how good your training program is or how motivated you are at the start. If you don't stick to it you're not going to get the results. I've built several elements into the *Beginner's Luck* program to increase its stick-to-ability.

The Golden Key and the Cat Levels are important adherence features, but the Beginner's Luck Facebook group seems to be a real winner when it comes to maintaining the motivation. Whether you've had a triumph or a disaster, sharing it with hundreds of other beginners who have likely experienced the same emotions is powerful. You're a part of something here, and whilst running is a very solitary sport being able to share your journey with other people who get it can help keep you accountable and focused.

If you're not on Facebook I can highly recommend creating a separate email account so you can set up a profile without danger of 'being found' by friends you'd rather not be found by. Go to www.facebook.com/groups/beginnersluck and treat the group as a forum that you can choose to observe from the sidelines or dive into head first.

Progress

When I was eight years old my dad used to take me out running during his lunch breaks. He was in the army so sport and fitness were a big part of his life and during those early days he taught me a lot about running. One of the things that I remember enjoying most about running was that I made really fast progress.

One week I was doing just a mile or two with him then very soon we were covering five or six. My dad told me that it was because with running you can guarantee you'll get better at it if you just keep doing it. Well that was good enough for me.

In reality this isn't strictly true – at some point just going out and running probably won't be enough for us to see continual improvements. But when you're just starting out it's not uncommon to see really fast development.

Non-linear

This early success can be something of a double-edged sword. On the one hand it's super-motivating to see how quickly you progress but on the other hand it can be hard to accept when this progress starts to slow down. When you start running, lots of changes take place in your body. We talked about adaptation and the importance of recovery earlier in the chapter and this is happening to lots of your systems.

– Your muscles get stronger and more efficient at processing the by-products of physical work (like lactic acid).

– Your respiratory system becomes more efficient: you start to draw more air into your lungs and get better at exchanging the oxygen for the carbon dioxide in your blood.

– The ligaments and tendons that run through your body and hold your bones and muscles together become stronger.

– Your nervous system gets more efficient at transmitting the signals from the brain to the muscles telling them when to fire.

– Even your hormones adapt to your running and you become better at using hormones like cortisol, adrenaline and insulin.

Lots of these adaptations happen very quickly (especially the changes to the neural system) but they don't continue to progress at this early rate. This is borne out in the program. From week 1 to week 3 you increase your total number of minutes running from seven to 24. That's an increase of almost 350%!

Over the next three weeks, however, the increase is from 25 to 40 minutes, or a 160% increase. Sure, there are a few other factors in there including the amount of rest taken between runs, but the point is that you'll make big leaps forward in the early stages with diminishing returns as you get deeper in. As long as you're gradually making progress, it's all good.

Remember, this program is about teaching you how to establish the habit of running, how to listen to your body and how to steadily build up your confidence as a runner. Understanding how your body adapts to your training should help you stay motivated even when you stop making such quantum leaps forward in your progress.

Time vs distance

Even if your ultimate goal is to run a 5k, a 10k, or further, at the start stick to time as your measure of progress. By all means keep an eye on how far you go each time but don't fall into the trap that a lot of runners do of equating higher mileage with better running. It's simply not the case and the temptation is to increase your pace beyond that which will allow you to complete the session comfortably.

All of my programs, including the 10k, half and full marathon programs, utilise time as the measure of progress instead of distance.

Two types of time
In the program there are two types of time that are of interest. The first is the number of minutes you are actually running for, and the second is the total length of time the session will take.

I've included both of these times in the program in Chapter 12 so you can see how much work you have to get through each session. Although I've only included the time of the actual session on the program, you should add five minutes to the start which should be a brisk walk to help warm up, and at least five minutes to the end after your last run. More on that in Chapter 5.

You can add more than five minutes to the start and finish if you like, but five is the minimum so you'll need to add at least 10 minutes to all the times in the program to figure out how long you need to complete each session.

Landmarks

The *Beginner's Luck* program is designed to help you get from scratch to running for an hour. This is a good length of time to say you can run for continuously, but so too is 45 minutes. 30 minutes isn't bad either, and hey, if you can't even run for the bus right now I'll bet you'll be pretty pleased when you can run for 10 minutes straight.

"I am so much more confident and happy that I no longer feel like I am rubbish at running. Also really proud of myself for getting to a stage where I can run for 45 minutes without stopping."
– Emma Cox

Take a look at the program and identify which sessions are going to see you break through various landmarks. Think about your reasons for wanting to run an hour. It's almost certainly an internal motivation: I imagine you'll feel like you've achieved something; done what you set out to do. Try and tie the same feeling of success into hitting these landmarks along the way.

If you've tried running in the past and couldn't get beyond a certain point, you know that when you cruise past it in the *Beginner's Luck* program you're going to be feeling pretty smug. Acknowledge these feelings of success and use them to help keep you motivated.

The 60 minute mark itself isn't an ultimate destination; in some ways it just represents a particular level of ability. But you can be sure that before you even make it there you'll be looking for the next challenge.

Skipping sessions

Thanks to the way the program is set out with extendable weeks, you never have to worry about skipping runs. If you miss a run for any reason at all, you simply do it the next day. Or the next, or the next. If you leave it more than a few days you may decide to go back and repeat the one you have already done before moving on again. You have to pass through each of the 10 Levels and 30 runs in the *Beginner's Luck* program to reach the end.

The only exception to this is if you are already comfortable with running for a few minutes at a time in which case I would recommend starting at a Level you are 100% confident you can comfortably complete. Without the preceding Levels you'll be giving your body a sudden challenge which may cause it to break if you're not careful.

The program

Beginner's Luck is designed for complete beginners who want to be able to run non-stop for 60 minutes. You may already be able to run for 5 to 10 minutes (or further) without taking a break, or you may find you struggle with even reaching the minute on, two minutes off in the first week.

This doesn't matter: in *Beginner's Luck* you progress at your own pace. Remember, just because it's a 10 week program doesn't mean everybody will take this exact length of time to get to 60 minutes of non-stop running.

The real objective of the program is to guide you on a journey of non-runner to runner.

To help you create the habit of running and build it into your life.

To teach you to love running for the sake of it, with all the challenges and sense of achievement that go with it.

The program is designed to give you the tools you need to continue doing this for 10 weeks, 10 months, 10 years and beyond.

The learning curve of the next 10 weeks is going to be steep. Some days will go better than others and I'm sure there will be times you want to quit. If you've tried and failed in the past you might be starting off on the back foot, but just remember that you ARE NOT your past failures.

This time you've got *Beginner's Luck.*

Chapter 3 – What kit do I really need?

One of the most appealing things about running, when compared to other sports, is the minimal amount of kit you need to get started. People say that all you need is a good-fitting pair of trainers and off you go. I'd say that you don't even need this! I'll come back to trainers in a minute, but in this chapter I'm going to cover kit you need to get started, what to spend your money on to help make the process more comfortable, and an insight into the crazy world of 'running accessories'.

Incidentally, when I refer to 'trainers' I'm talking about sports shoes, not horse trainers or personal trainers. Whenever I present in Ireland I have to remember to refer to these as 'runners', whereas in the UK this would be taken to mean 'people who run'. All very confusing, but from now on I'll refer only to trainers and you'll know what I mean!

The basics

Given that running in the nude is an arrestable offence I'm going to assume that you're going to be wearing clothes of some description when you run. One of the things that puts off beginner runners is thinking that they have to go out and buy a load of brightly-coloured Lycra before setting foot outside for their first run.

The truth is that you probably already have everything you need right there in your wardrobe, so let's get rid of that excuse right now.

When you start running, the very first changes that will take place in your body are neurological. You are going to get a bit fitter, but the initial progress will come from your body and brain 'learning' how to run. At some point it's a good idea to invest in some kit – more of that in a minute – but to start with just find something you feel comfortable in so you can get out there for the first runs and start to benefit from these early adaptations.

A pair of jogging bottoms or loose fitting trousers and a comfortable top is a good starting point. Clothes you feel comfortable wearing will make the experience so much more enjoyable in the critical early stages when you're still making up your mind whether this is something you can stick with or not. The last thing you want is to feel self-conscious, so wear what you like and don't worry about not looking 'like a runner'.

If it's raining, a waterproof jacket is a good idea but, once again, just grab what you already have. Hat, gloves, scarf... wrap up and then get out there to do battle with the elements.

The elephant in the room when we talk about basic kit requirements is what you put on your feet so let's address that now.

Trainers

It really is worth getting a properly-fitted pair of trainers as early as you can in your running career. You don't have to get them immediately, but neither should you leave it too long before getting fitted out.

After a lifetime of walking in a certain way and wearing different types of shoes (heels in particular, ladies) your feet will have adopted a certain way of moving. Your arches may drop in or they may be particularly high. You may have restrictions in your big toe joints which cause a roll of the foot to occur. There could be ankle immobility that changes the function of the foot or perhaps you tend to favour the outside or inside of your foot as you walk.

You may not be aware of any of these things during your day-to-day activities, but when you start to run you multiply the forces, at the same time as increasing the frequency with which they occur.

Trainers are designed to help your feet track more efficiently, which is why there seems to be such a dauntingly large range of different designs and brands. Oh, and then you'll get the group of runners who tell you that wearing 'foot coffins' is the last thing you should be doing and barefoot running is the way forward...

I'm starting to feel a little anxious just writing about this so I can only imagine what it must look like when you feel you're entering a whole new world. It could be enough to put you off before even starting so, once again, let's demolish that barrier.

To start with, just stick anything comfortable on your feet. If you don't own a pair of trainers you might want to consider getting a 'proper' pair right away, but you can get away with buying a basic pair of non-run-specific trainers. The faster you progress through the program the sooner you'll need to get yourself kitted out with the right footwear, but to start with just get out there and get cracking.

Once you move into Lynx Week and you're racking up more than 20 minutes of running for each session it's time to start paying more attention to your feet. Get yourself down to a specialist running shop like Sweatshop, Up & Running or one of the many independent retailers and speak to one of the sales team.

They tend to be runners themselves and understand your needs far better than just the sales person you'd meet walking into a generic sportswear shop. They should listen to the kind of running you're doing, take a look at the way you run (either on a treadmill for a minute or so, or just up and down the shop) then give you two or three pairs of shoes to try on.

If they use language like motion control, cushioned, pronation or foot strike just ask them to explain what they mean and how it relates to you. Shoe geeks can get a bit carried away so don't be afraid to bring them back down to your level of understanding. If they can't explain what the benefits of the shoe are in layman's terms there is a chance they are just regurgitating what they read on the sales course and don't really understand it at all.

A higher price doesn't necessarily indicate a better pair of trainers, so just go with what fits well and feels comfortable. If you've never worn running shoes before it'll feel like you have a pair of clouds strapped to your feet and a little smile may just dart across your face as you imagine getting out there for the next Cat.

Sports bra

I mentioned that there was very little in the way of 'essential' kit for runners, but if you're a lady then a good quality, well-fitted sports bra fits squarely in that category. Sports tops with in-built bras aren't good enough – you need to get yourself some support that reduces the bounce and prevents irreparable damage to the delicate Cooper's ligaments that hold your breasts in place. Once these become stretched and damaged there's no going back so take care of your boobs.

A good sports bra should feel much tighter than your normal bras because they have a much tougher job to do in contending with the amplified up and down movement of running. Sports bra manufacturers like LessBounce and Shock Absorber design their products to minimise unwanted movement and make your running more comfortable.

Investing in kit

Although it's not essential, having proper running kit really does make a difference to your comfort, your experience, and your motivation. Most of it won't make you run any faster but anything that encourages you to get out more often to train is going to help you transition from beginner to confident runner.

So when you're ready to invest in a bit of kit, here's what I recommend you start off with.

1) Technical t-shirts

Just about every running t-shirt these days is made from so-called technical fabric that will help wick the sweat away from your body. Cotton tends to hold the sweaty material against your skin which can get a bit uncomfortable. Running t-shirts also tend to have more attention to details such as where the seams are (to avoid chaffing), fit, and reflective material for safety.

A loose fitting, long- or short-sleeved t-shirt could be a running top all by itself or you could use it as a base-layer for those colder runs.

2) Bottoms

This is a matter of preference, but you're looking at either shorts, 'capris' or tights. Running shorts will once again be made of wicking fabric, whilst capris (three quarter length tights) and tights will be a tighter material like Lycra. Guys, the tights aren't just for the ladies. They're great when it's a bit colder and you get some compression benefits as well. There should be a law against guys wearing obscenely short running shorts but you can get ones that come a little further down the thigh which are far more respectable if you're not ready to rock the men-in-tights look quite yet.

3) Warm tops

If you're running in colder conditions you want to layer up your clothes. A wicking t-shirt will act as a base-layer (though true base-layers tend to be a bit tighter and even lighter weight than a regular running t-shirt) and then on top you could wear a lightweight running fleece. Tops with a half zip are good because you can regulate how much heat they hold in as you warm up yourself.

4) Running jacket

Something water- and wind-resistant is good, though some will make you sound like you're wearing a crisp packet as you run. Test a few out in the shop – these can be quite expensive pieces of kit but a good jacket will become your best friend on cold and wet runs.

5) Socks

Yes, there are even special running socks! They tend to be 'left and right' like your trainers, so they fit your feet better and cause fewer hot spots that could lead to blisters. Normal sports socks are fine in most cases though.

Some pieces of kit can seem really expensive. There's no need to pay top dollar for the best there is, but one or two pieces of really good quality gear will pay you back ten-fold in the years it'll last you. I still have a running jacket I bought seven years ago and it's like having a hug from an old friend every time I zip it up.

If you're on a budget, try supermarket own-brands as these are often far better than the price would suggest, but then that's marketing for you. Aldi is renowned for producing decent quality, but rock bottom price kit so take a look.

Accessories

I was wandering around a running show a few months ago (yes, a running show – I'm telling you, this is a whole new world you're stepping into here!) and was blown away by the amount of 'stuff' out there ready to part you from your money.

In fact, I came away from the visit with problems that I didn't even know I had two hours previously.

Let's just say there is an almost inexhaustible selection of accessories you could buy. Don't let that put you off trying some of them out, just get the important stuff first. I'm sure that Nip Guards and teeny tiny tubs of petroleum jelly are exactly what some runners are looking for but your money may be better spent on your key pieces of kit first.

Watches

The first accessory runners tend to focus on is their watch. A digital watch that tells the time and has a stopwatch will set you back about a tenner, but when you start researching you'll find watches that only just stop short of doing the running itself for you. I'm being facetious here: a good running watch can add a whole other dimension to your experience but I'm yet to be convinced that knowing the exact Cartesian co-ordinates every step of the way is an essential feature.

Having an interval timer on a watch is a bonus as it allows you to 'program' in things like three minutes on, 90 seconds off. You just set it up to beep at each interval so you don't then have to be constantly looking down at your wrist. Loads of sports watches will have this functionality (you're looking for 'timer' as well as 'stopwatch' in the list of features) and you should expect to pay around £40-£50 for one. Be warned though: I've never had one of these watches that has lasted for more than 18 months as something always seems to go wrong.

The next step up is to get a watch with GPS. Just like your car's sat nav, this will allow you to monitor in real time how far you have run and how fast you are doing it. This has tremendous appeal to some runners whilst for others it's just another meaningless distraction. For a watch with basic GPS capabilities you should expect to pay £100 but the fancier ones are closer to £300. Unless you're an alpine adventurer, however, you probably won't get close to using the full functionality of these monsters.

Most of these watches don't stop working when your run finishes. You can then plug them directly into your computer to analyse the data, compare to previous runs, map out exactly where you've been and upload to your social media profiles... and take a breath!

Smart phones and apps

You may own a smart phone, in which case you already possess a whole heap of potential running accessories and you don't even know it yet! You can download apps that do almost the same as a GPS watch, or just time your intervals. Many beginner runners find the Gymboss app really useful for telling you when it's time to run or walk.

If you're carrying a smart phone you'll need some kind of accessory to secure it to your body. I wouldn't recommend holding it in your hand as it's easy to drop, but a neoprene waist pack or arm band are simple solutions. Do a bit of research and you'll find plenty of options to try out, but I've included a couple in the Resources section at the back to give you an idea.

Heart rate monitors

The technology doesn't stop with measuring how fast you are running; it can also measure how fast your heart is beating. Heart Rate Monitors (HRMs) have been around for quite a while now and whilst you can pick up a basic model for under £30 they are far from essential.

It can be useful to know what your HR is when you run, but only in relation to pre-determined heart rate zones. Usually these are estimated based on your age but as this can be wildly inaccurate it can alter the effectiveness of your training.

Besides, in the *Beginner's Luck* program we're more concerned with holding a slow pace you can hold a conversation at. You don't need a HRM to determine this – go by how you feel.

Weatherproof your running

As well as a good rain jacket, there are a few other items of kit you might want to invest in if you're running in inclement weather conditions. Putting on the right kit for the conditions makes you feel like a warrior getting dressed to go out to do battle with Mother Nature.

My mum always told me there was no such thing as bad weather, only Southerners. So if you're not from Oop North here are a few more choice items to arm yourself with to weatherproof your running.

Hat and gloves. Any old hat and gloves will do to start with, but something lighter weight and water resistant is a good idea if you often find yourself out there in the rain. My hands get really cold when I run and it makes it unpleasant for me so I always wear something on my hands unless it's above 5°. I'm less bothered about a hat, but all of this is down to personal preference.

Many runners prefer to wear just a headband that covers their ears but not their head. Others like neck warmers... Whatever you need to do to stop the weather becoming an excuse. If it's really throwing it down just accept that you're going to get a bit wet. Just remember, skin is waterproof.

Music whilst you run

The subject of listening to music seems to divide runners. Some say they can't run without it, others say it's a terrible distraction. Neither is right or wrong, although many road races are now banning the use of headphones as they are causing runners to be unaware of dangers and safety warnings from marshals.

For now, you might just want to try with and without to see which camp you fall into.

If you do decide to listen to music you'll need an mp3 player, some way of attaching it to your body, and a pair of headphones. A smart phone is an easy option for an mp3 player though they can be a bit bulky and you might not want to expose it to the elements. As you can also download timing apps like Gymboss to a smart phone to help you through the program, it becomes an all-in-one solution. Some phone manufacturers are even starting to build in fitness tracking facilities into the hardware of their handsets, such is the trend.

Whether you use your phone or a more compact mp3 player, there are a plethora of accessories designed to go round your arm or your waist to attach it to your body. I have included a couple of examples in the Resources section.

Getting a good pair of headphones is another good idea as you don't want them wriggling their way out of your ears at inopportune moments. Brands like Yurbuds (see the Resources section for the link) have developed headphones that 'lock' into place, have an almost unbreakable cord, and allow ambient sounds in so you can remain aware of your surroundings.

Easy motivation

Picture the last time you bought yourself a really nice outfit, pair of jeans or shoes. How did you feel when you looked at yourself in the mirror? Didn't you just want to get out there and wear your new getup? Of course you did! Running kit is no different. Investing in a few pieces of well-fitting clothes that you enjoy wearing is motivation in itself to get out there and run.

Some beginners have told me that they celebrate the completion of another level by going out and purchasing another running t-shirt or pair of leggings. When you've had to work hard for a particular item of clothing it takes on more meaning when you slip it on for your next run!

Wish lists

When you're ready, get yourself a couple of key pieces that aren't going to break the bank. Then whenever you find something you really like but can't justify buying right away, add it to your wish list. When it's Christmas or your birthday rolls around, point your nearest and dearest in the direction of your special list and you're guaranteed to get something you really want.

George Anderson

Chapter 4 – How do I stay motivated to run?

One of the things I really wanted to understand was what the major challenges and 'blocks' were for beginner runners. What had stopped them being successful in the past? What did they need support on this time round to make it stick?

I asked this question to the group of beginners testing the program and they nearly all came back with the same answer: mind-set and motivation.

How do you not give up? How do you transition from 'non-runner' to habitual and happy runner?

If you've tried to get into running in the past and then quit, it's likely that your brain is going to remember this past experience. "Running is hard", or "I'm a terrible runner", or "I CAN'T run" are all common stories we tell ourselves.

"I am so proud of how I stuck at it, managed it and knew I can do it. I feel amazing: never thought I could run, but I can!"
– Joanna Garnett

"It feels great to have got this far. Honestly, if you told me that I would be running for one hour I would have laughed. The huge sense of personal satisfaction and enjoyment. I feel so proud of myself. And I now find myself maybe not wanting to go on and run a marathon but do more around my pace and run a 10k race!"
– Elaine McGauran

Tell yourself these stories often enough and build up enough evidence to support your argument and you'll never move beyond the embryonic stages of running. You'll start believing it and then you have no chance.

Thing is, most of the stories we tell ourselves are fairy tales, otherwise known as opinions. In our *opinion* running is hard, or we're terrible at it, or we just can't do it. These aren't facts, they're perceptions. Facts are irrefutable but opinions can be (and often are) proved wrong.

You can change your story, but for this to happen you have to be ready to stop running in the past and acknowledge this critical difference between fact and opinion.

As I'm sure you know, the definition of insanity is doing the same thing over again and expecting a different result. Clearly, trying to do the exact same thing that you did last time you tried to run isn't going to work. But that's okay because this time you have *Beginner's Luck.*

The voice inside your head

Sometimes I feel like I'm going mad when I run. Maybe you have experienced it before as well – you get those little voices inside your head trying to pull you in different directions.

"You can do this!" says the good voice.

"Oh my God this hurts, just stop and the pain will go away!", or "Why on earth are you doing this to yourself?", chimes in the bad voice a little later on when things are starting to get tough.

It's like a constant battle, an argument going on inside your head, and sometimes it really does feel as though you're going crazy. Let me tell you now: you're never going to silence the negative self-talk. I've been running for years and the voices inside my head are still there, shouting just as loudly as they always have been. You can never make them go away entirely, you just need to learn how to embrace them, see them for what they are, and make that the positive voice shout louder.

This takes practice and you're bound to have a few tears along the way where the self-doubting, bad-mouthing negative voice reigns supreme. Yet again it'll be proved correct. You stop, you quit, you throw your trainers in the bin and swear you're never going to go running again.

These are just episodes along the way, they're not the end. You just need to get back in the saddle and have another crack at it. And the next time you'll be a little more prepared for the voices, but they'll always be there.

I've been running for nearly 30 years and I still get those horrible little voices in my head that ask me why the hell I'm doing this.

"I mean come on; I'm not exactly enjoying this right now am I? Not right at this moment; I don't need this. Come on, slow down or take a break..."

You're never going to silence them completely but you can certainly learn to ignore them. Practise turning up the volume on your positive self-talk and drown out the negativity. Become your own coach. Motivate yourself. Shout at yourself (in your head or out loud; it's up to you). Do whatever you need to do but just remember: they are only voices, and not real people with any kind of authority, so you don't have to listen to them.

If you'd like to read more about how to improve your relationship with these voices then I can highly recommend Dr Steve Peters' book The Chimp Paradox. In this book he brilliantly explains how our Inner Chimp may seem to be setting you on a path to self-destruct, but in fact always has your best interests at heart.

There will be plenty of ah-ha moments as you read the book and start to make sense of some of your behaviours and actions.

What's your WHY?

If someone asks you why you've taken up running you'll probably spin some easy line like it's just something you've always wanted to do. You might say other stuff but really, deep down it doesn't even come close to your real WHY. Your WHY is your ultimate, most powerful, deep-rooted reason for wanting to run. You may have to dig around a little to find it: you definitely have one (nobody is forcing you to run, right?) but you may never have spoken or written down what it is.

Some people run because they feel it's a part of their identity. Some because it presents a challenge they can work towards overcoming, which in turn allows them to feel a sense of achievement.

Some people run because they think it'll be a convenient way to lose weight. But there are plenty of other ways of losing weight, so why running? What's the *deep* reason for wanting to run? I'll wait here until you've worked out what yours is. Work it out; then write it down.

Figured it out yet?

Okay, good. Because this is what will keep you going when the voices start arguing or you find yourself debating whether you're going to head out the door today.

If you want to read more on this subject then I can recommend Simon Sinek's excellent book Start With Why. It's a bit businessy but still packed with plenty of self-development concepts that expand on the few words I've written here.

Understand the sacrifices

Time

If we assume that you're planning on hitting all three runs each week, that's three lots of 30 to 60 minutes you need to carve out of your already busy life. Every week. You can't just add them in; you need to take something out as well.

Starting to run might mean getting up half an hour earlier (and sacrificing sleep). You might go for a run in your lunch break instead of working through (that work isn't going to just get done by itself now, is it?). Maybe you go for a run in the evening and sacrifice family or social time.

Understand how it's going to fit into your life right from the start and then you won't be surprised when you suddenly have to be more organised.

Relationships

Hopefully you won't have to sacrifice any relationships, but there's a chance that several of them may change. It's likely that friends or family will be affected by your new 'hobby'. You're going to be disappearing out the door two or three times a week to spend time (very selfishly) on your own. You need to square this with your significant other(s) so you get the support you're going to need along the way.

You'll be wearing different clothes, talking a different language (it won't be long before you're dropping words like "fartlek" and "lactic threshold" into conversation), maybe even eating different foods. People will notice. You may start turning down dinner invites because you have a run planned for that night. Or you're out at the pub on Saturday night but you can't drink as much as you used to because you have to get up early on Sunday morning and nail that Tiger 3 session.

Things are going to change so you need to make sure the people who are going to be affected are on board.

Saboteurs and cheerleaders

They say that you are the average of the five people you spend most of your time with. If you hang around with negative, pessimistic people all day long you can't help but have similar thoughts. Likewise, when you surround yourself with positive people who actively pursue their goals and ambitions, I'm sure you can imagine: some of it will rub off on you.

We call these two groups Cheerleaders and Saboteurs and it's important that you understand how to recognise them.

Cheerleaders

These are the guys and gals you want to be hanging around with. They're the ones who will get in your corner right from the start, unconditionally supporting you even if you have a track record of trying these things and not continuing. It's important to surround yourself with these friends as they're the ones who will be the first to pick you up when the going gets tough and the first to congratulate you on your mini-victories along the way.

They may be runners themselves but they don't have to be. The advantage of finding running-cheerleaders is that they will understand where you're coming from. They'll encourage you to just get out there and enjoy it for the sake of it. You'll get advice and tips from them that, even if you don't take, will make you feel like you're being listened to. Like you have someone else on your side rooting for you.

Make a list of these friends and make a conscious effort to spend time with them. You don't have to talk about running all the while with them (that'll get old really quickly) but just having them close by will have a positive effect.

Saboteurs

The sad thing about this group of friends and family members is that they usually don't realise the harm their comments do.

"Oh here we go, how long will it last this time?", or "Go on, just one more drink: I'm sure it won't matter if you miss your little run tomorrow."

Yeah, thanks for that. Although saboteurs have different reasons for their lack of support, it often boils down to insecurity. Not many of us particularly relish change, so when it's right there in your face because your best mate's onto his or her next crazy exercise fad it can make us a little insecure.

"What's wrong with the way things are?" Or, "Now she's taken up jogging, I suppose she thinks she's better than the rest of us", for example.

It's pretty easy to categorise this group of people but unfortunately not quite so easy to avoid spending time with them. If they're in your close circle of friends or immediate family you'll inevitably be spending time with them during the week. The closer they are to you the more important it is that you sit down and talk to them about how this is important to you and that you would appreciate their support.

Try and get to the bottom of where their negativity is coming from, and explain how their comments are affecting you. You could even invite them to join you!

Wherever possible, minimise the time you spend with saboteurs. Work colleagues and peripheral friends should be avoided when you're trying to establish a habit. At that point you'll be most sensitive to their negative rubbish so make your excuses and don't spend more time with them than is necessary.

If talk does turn to your running endeavours, play it down as much as possible and move on to a different subject. This might all sound a bit extreme but I've seen people brought down by negative friends over and over again. Strive to spend as much of your time with the five people you would like to become the average of.

Enjoy the journey

You've set yourself a goal of running for X amount of minutes (this is a 0-60 minute running program after all!) or Y miles. When you get there, job done. Mission accomplished. Celebration time. But to think like that is to miss half the point about running.

Running isn't about a destination unless you're being chased by an angry bear, in which case the destination is the safety of your house. All other times the runs you do are an end in themselves. Each time you go out for a run you are achieving something with that very act. You're experiencing something. You'll be a different person at the end of the run compared with the beginning; forever growing, learning and developing.

Runners are a funny bunch. We make jokes about the pain, the loneliness, the weather, the ridiculousness of running. But there's something deep down that keeps us coming back for more and it's not just the promise of being able to run further or faster.

I did a straw poll survey on Facebook of runners. I asked them, if they knew 100% that they would never get any better at running, would they still continue to get out there to train and race. Every single one of them came back and said 'yes'.

You don't need to just understand this, you need to believe it. Not because I say so, but because you're going to look deep inside yourself and figure it out on your own.

Get your kit out!

I love running early in the morning. It's just such a wonderful time of day to be out there, ruling the world. When my alarm goes off at 5am though, I don't always immediately feel this way. So what I try to do is generate a little enthusiasm in advance, create some good intentions the night before and harness them the following morning.

By getting my kit out the night before and mentally rehearsing the run I create a powerful feeling tied into an image of my kit. I imagine myself waking up, getting changed, doing my pre-run warm up routine and heading out for the route I've planned. I imagine how amazing it's going to feel and how much I'm going to enjoy it when I'm out there.

Then when I wake up in the morning, not only is my kit already sitting there waiting for me to put it on, but I can also easily bring back those feelings of excitement and motivation for the run.

Keep it interesting

One thing you definitely want to avoid is getting bored with your running. To begin with everything will be new. Running is a great way to see your world from a different viewpoint. You can drive down a street a hundred times but when you run along the pavements you really get to know it.

But if you always repeat the same route your mind soon gets bored. It becomes less stimulating and you become less inspired to go out and run again. Change the route regularly – try different circuits, the out and back, or even the out *or* back methods described in Chapter 1.

Run with somebody

This can be another double-edged sword, but as long as you find somebody who is at just about the same ability as yourself it can be very effective as a motivational strategy. In fact, you can help motivate each other, especially if you agree in advance to meet at a certain time for a run. You wouldn't want to let each other down now would you?

Problems can arise when your running buddy is slightly more advanced than you. When this happens there's a tendency for them to drag you round that little bit faster than is good for you. You'll end up feeling as though you're holding them back and motivation will start to move in the opposite direction. Likewise, if you're the fitter partner your progress will be stunted by having to slow down or take extra breaks whilst you wait.

There are plenty of advantages to running with somebody so you'll need to try it out for yourself. It's a great chance to socialise whilst doing something healthy but do keep trying to make progress through the program.

Dealing with a lack of progress

In the early stages of your running you are likely to make progress in leaps and bounds. As your body goes through the initial stages of adaptation you'll find that this progress slows down and occasionally seems to grind to a halt.

There are a number of reasons for this but I'll get to that in a moment. First of all, let's deal with the feelings you'll experience and the thoughts you'll have if and when this happens. Okay, let's stop beating around the bush: this WILL happen at some point, otherwise we'd all just keep on getting better and better and the Olympics would be an altogether different affair.

The real frustration is when these 'plateaus' kick in before you feel they're due. You'll probably say things like, "What's the point? I'm going through all this pain and still not getting any better." The old demons will rear their heads again and tell you things like, "I *knew* you'd fail – when are you going to learn that you're *not a runner*?"

You need to acknowledge these voices (go back and re-read the bit about 'the voices in your head' from earlier in this chapter) and then just move on.

Consider how you are measuring your progress. Don't just go by how quickly you're moving through the program. How are you feeling? Are you noticing any changes in your body?

Are you becoming more confident with your running? Has your diet also improved? How about your energy levels?

Is there any reason why you *have* to progress to the next level? What's the worst that would happen if you were stuck where you were for a couple of weeks? You're still getting out there running and I'll bet that's more than you were doing before.

Plateaus happen for a number of reasons. Sometimes it's because your body is just taking a little longer to adapt and sometimes it's because you're trying to run a little faster than you should. Remember, the faster you run the less time you'll be able to sustain it for. I've seen hundreds of runners break through a continuous-minutes-run plateau just by slowing down.

Please believe that a plateau is something to be broken through; it's not some kind of limit.   You can't afford to let the voices get to you now, not when you've already got this far.

Final word on motivation

Everybody is motivated by different things. To add even more complication, what motivates you now won't motivate you in six months' or even six weeks' time. You need to continuously dig deep, recognise that your mojo will ebb and flow and learn how to ride it.

Keep on believing, and keep on running.

Chapter 5 – What is the best way to warm up and cool down?

It's 6am. Your alarm goes off and you swing your legs out of bed, stumble downstairs and pull on your running gear. As you're tying the laces of your running shoes you yawn and feel a few vertebrae click satisfyingly in your back. It feels good so when you stand back up again you give your body a bit more of a stretch like an old cat. You shake your arms, unlock the front door and head out for your run.

For most people who run in the mornings, that just about sums up the pre-run routine but it's far from ideal. When you go from lying or sitting (i.e. after a long day in the office) to running, your body needs to acclimatise to the new position and the increased demands you're placing on it.

Preparing properly for each run will make it more enjoyable, improve your performance (in other words make it feel easier!) and reduce the chances of picking up an injury.

The pre-run walk

Each session on the program has a number of minutes of running, and a number of minutes walking. Before you start your first burst of running, however, you should complete a minimum of five, ideally 10, minutes of walking. This does two things. Firstly, it helps to loosen up the legs, taking them through a very similar range of movement that you'll be asking of them when it comes time to run. Secondly, this initial walk marks the start of 'me-time'.

Running is an amazing way to spend quality time with yourself. Life is full of demands, pressures and other people needing attention. Often we put ourselves at the bottom of the priority list. When you're out for your run, *you* are number one. The walk at the start of the run is the time when you spend a few moments getting into your own space, temporarily putting the rest of your life and responsibilities on hold and focusing on the task in hand.

Spending these few precious minutes alone with your thoughts can become an important part of your week and is one of the reasons why running is such a good stress-buster. Even when you have progressed to a level of fitness that means you no longer have to walk at the start, you'll still start the session off with an easy jog as your body adapts and you get into the right frame of mind.

Pre-run stretching

There is no evidence to support the notion that a general, pre-workout session of stretching where the muscles are held for a few seconds has any bearing on reducing your risk of injury. In fact, some studies have shown that for more extreme versions of running like sprinting and hurdling, too much static stretching at the start can actually increase the risk of injury as it reduces the natural springiness of the muscles.

A few years ago I used to teach various modules on gym instructor and personal trainer diploma courses. At gym instructor level it is still a requirement to teach a pre-exercise stretch, but I always used to teach it just enough so that I could easily un-teach it when they later came to do their PT diplomas.

Whilst a whole body stretch really isn't necessary, if you are aware of tightness in specific areas then a bit of a stretch can help ease it off and give you more confidence on your run.

The exception to this 'no stretching strategy' is the hip flexors, which I believe everybody should stretch before heading out the door. These muscles run between the thigh bone, the pelvis and lower back. They commonly get tight when you spend a lot of time sitting down, which means that when you then stand up (or run) they are slightly shorter and so pull on the points they are attached to.

As the hip flexors pull on the pelvis, this whole structure is rotated so as to cause your bottom to stick out a bit more. It may not even be noticeable to the eye, but it certainly will be to your hamstrings.

Many runners complain of tight hamstrings and calves and these are common areas for injury. But if the muscle is being stretched due to the pelvis being rotated out of alignment then no amount of stretching is going to solve the problem. In fact, it could even make it worse.

Stretching out the hip flexors can help to take this strain out of the hamstrings and calves.

Similarly, with the back. Because one part of the hip flexor attaches to the lower spine, if it becomes tight it can cause misalignment in this area too. The lumbar area of the spine is a key structure in load-bearing and transmitting forces up and down the body. So an imbalance here is likely to cause problems either immediately, or later on down the line.

So, I think we can agree then: it's worth spending a few moments stretching out these troublesome muscles! And the great news is that it's also quite straightforward to do. Simply kneel on one knee with the opposite foot about 18" out in front, then drive your front knee forwards and tilt the tailbone underneath like a pelvic thrust.

There is a link in the resources section to the website where I have shot a video explaining exactly how to perform this stretch.

You should feel an immediate stretch in the front of your back leg, right around the hip area. Hold this stretch for a few seconds, back off and then go back into it again. Continue this pulsing movement for 30 seconds to a minute and then repeat on the other side.

Simple, yet ridiculously effective. I can't remember the last time I did any kind of workout without first having done this. If I was faced with an angry lion, I would still first consider if I had a few seconds just to loosen off my hip flexors before running in the opposite direction (I'm sure he'd wait).

Foam rolling

The slightly odd pastime of foam rolling has gained in popularity in recent years and made the transition from the therapist's clinic to front rooms across the land in much the same way the Swiss ball did a couple of decades previously.

A foam roller is a length of high density foam, usually about 6" in diameter, that you lie on with various parts of your body and roll up and down. I'm not going to lie to you. Foam rolling can feel like self-torture at times but the fact remains that it is an effective pre- and post-run strategy.

As you pass the roller over the length of the muscle it massages out knots, allowing it to lengthen naturally. I mention foam rolling in this book not as an attempt to teach you how to do it properly, but merely to introduce you to the concept. Ironing out tight spots in muscles before you run can help tune up your body, and repeating it afterwards can aid recovery. There are plenty of good books on the subject of foam rolling and I even include an entire video module in my half and full marathon programs. I have included a short video with some of my favourite pain-inducing-recovery-accelerating foam rolling moves on the companion website (www.runningbygeorge.com/beginners/foamroller)

For some of you, reading this may pique your interest. In which case go forth on a quest of further discovery. For others it may lodge somewhere in your brain but not be acted upon until you come across it again from a different source. Others still will have been put off as soon as they read "self-torture" and seek no further learning. Either way, there's plenty of other good stuff to be getting your teeth stuck into!

Mobility

I remember doing my very first fitness qualification at Leicester College in 2000 and we were learning about mobilisation exercises. They had us walking on a treadmill 'warming up' whilst we rolled our shoulders in larger and larger circles until we were 'brushing our ears with our biceps' and 'painting wheels on a wagon with our fingers'. I don't think I ever got a single client to do this particular drill as it just looked plain ridiculous but the foundation of mobility had been set.

You know how you wake up in the morning and spring out of bed fresh as a daisy? No, neither do I. It takes a while for your body to wake up and a part of this process is your joints mobilising. They have a fluid in them that becomes quite viscous when there has been no movement for a while and they are cold, so mobilisation helps them move more freely.

Look at a cat or dog the next time they wake from a sleep. First thing they do is give it a big old stretch and shake their whole body out before mooching off in search of food. They do this for the same reason: their joints become stiff and they need to mobilise them before they start to function effectively.

For runners, mobilisation is important because if we just head off for a trot without paying any attention to how our joints are functioning we're going to be in for a rough ride. On the *Beginner's Luck* program there is a walk warm-up built into every session. This will certainly help loosen things off, but we also want to get the spine mobilised and for that we have to go 3D.

3D spine mobility

Your spine is a clever bit of kit and it's worth looking after. Even a few moments spent mobilising it every day – in particular before an exercise session – can help keep it supple and doing its job with the minimum of fuss. We already talked about how stretching out the hip flexors is important thanks to the muscle attachment to the lower back, but 3D mobility will take things right the way to the top.

The spine moves in 3 planes of movement: you can bend it forwards and back, side to side, and you can rotate it left and right. And that's pretty much the size of it when it comes to mobility as well.

Try gently rolling down, tucking your chin into your chest and then one vertebrae at a time with the knees slightly bent until you're as low as you can comfortably go. Let gravity do the work, hang there for a few moments and then gently climb back up again, finishing the movement off with a nice big back arch stretch. Do this a couple of times before moving onto the side bends.

For these, clasp your hands together over your head and push your hips out to the right whilst you lean over to the left. You should feel a stretch down the right side of your body which you want to hold for a moment and then move to the other side. Five to 10 of these big body yawns should do the trick to mobilise the spine in this plane of movement.

Finally, stand with your feet about twice hip-width apart and rotate your whole body to one side and then the other. Feel a nice big twist rise up through your hips and back, mobilising your spine in this plane of movement after about 5 to 10 rotations to each side.

All of these mobility drills should take approximately 90 seconds, so a minuscule investment for a nice big fat return in the make-my-running-easier stakes. There is a short video on the companion website that demonstrates each of these mobilisers: www.runningbygeorge.com/beginners/ mobilisers.

Post-run

When you come back from a run and you're tired, hot and sweaty, all you want to do is jump in the shower or have a sit down for a few minutes. To be fair, you have already spent a few minutes flushing out your muscles with that final period of walking we have built into each run. But an extra few minutes at the end of your session invested in post-run recovery will help your body adapt to the stresses you just put it through. Think of it like an extra 1% of effort to get an extra 25% return.

First of all, though, let's get one thing straight: no amount of stretching or foam rolling after a run is going to completely prevent muscle soreness. If you're going to get sore, you're going to get sore. These strategies can help but they won't completely stop that post-workout soreness.

Post-run stretching

Stretching muscles out after a run can help to return them to their original length after spending several minutes vigorously contracting. Spend a few minutes stretching out your hip flexors, hamstrings, glutes, calves and quads. Try to hold each stretch for at least 20 seconds and ideally closer to 1 minute. There is a video demonstration of each of these stretches at the companion website: www.runningbygeorge.com/beginners/stretches.

Post-run foam rolling

Just as rolling at the start of a run can help with your movement preparation and muscle function, post-run rolling can help release knots that may have appeared on the run. It may be painful immediately after the run so this is something you can leave for a few hours if you wish. If you're partial to a bit of television in the evening this is the perfect time to spend a more relaxed 10 to 20 minutes rolling out your weary legs.

Ice treatment

Ice is great for immediately applying to injuries, but it is also an excellent tool to speed up post-run recovery. There are different ways you can do this, but just like the foam rolling, expect to get friendly with pain and discomfort. The easiest way to apply ice is just with a bag of frozen peas on your most achy muscles and joints. It will help the inflammation go down and flood the area with fresh nutrient-rich blood when you remove the ice. 15 minutes at a time is the most you would need.

If you're feeling a little tougher, turn your shower to extra cold and for the first few minutes of your post-run wash and spray your legs with the freezing cold water. This really does work, but takes a bit of character.

For those of you feeling supremely hardcore, nothing quite beats an ice bath. We're not looking at full submersion here; just fill a bath with about 4-6" inches of water and then chuck in a couple of bags of ice before sitting in it for 5 to 10 minutes.

Which of these ice strategies you choose to adopt – if any – will depend on the balance you're looking to strike between results and sacrifice. Nobody enjoys an ice bath, but there's a reason that elite athletes regularly do it. Personally, I reserve them for after the toughest of runs or workouts, but the direct ice pack or cold shower I find much more manageable.

Chapter 6 – How do I avoid getting injured?

Having a niggly knee, tight calves or a sore foot doesn't normally bother most people more than a general awareness that something's not quite right. For a runner, however, the forces are amplified and it's one of the most frustrating things imaginable.

You *want* to run, but you *can't*. All those people sitting around all day on their couches without injuries but who *don't* want to run, even though they could if they wanted to; and there's you with all the motivation in the world but having to sit around at home feeling sorry for yourself.

Injured runners aren't pleasant people to be around, and although there's no way we can completely negate the possibility that it may happen to you one day, we can certainly take steps to reduce the chances. People (non-runners, usually) go to great lengths to tell you how bad running is for your knees and back, and how we're not designed to run. They're almost happy if you *do* get injured because it reinforces that they were, indeed, right all along.

How do you run?

Although we cover technique in Chapter 8, it's worth starting off this section with a nod to the way you run as it is rather important. Let's take a look at the key aspects of technique as related to injury prevention.

Posture

How you hold your body as you run is crucial to the way forces are transmitted through your bones and joints.

Concentrate on pulling your body up tall as you run, as though you had a piece of string attached to the top of your head. This will automatically draw in your tummy and activate your core without you having to think about it.

Activation

Although not strictly a technique issue, if certain muscles aren't working properly you will end up overusing other muscles when you run. A great example of this is the glutes (your bum) which we really *want* to be firing as you run, but in many cases are just there for the ride.

So to kick them into play we can activate them before we head out the front door. It's really easy to do, takes about a minute, and really works to wake them up so they have more of a chance to help you as you run.

Stand tall and simply squeeze your butt cheeks for all you're worth. As you squeeze them, for about 10 seconds repeatedly punch them with your fists. This sounds a bit weird, but the punching increases the signal from the brain to the muscle so it knows exactly which area to fire up. Do this for maybe three rounds of 10 seconds and you should feel them taking part a bit more on the run, taking some of the load off your poor old hamstrings. There is a video on the companion website that demonstrates this activation drill: www.runningbygeorge.com/beginners/activation.

Relaxed running

As you run, try to relax as much as possible; especially your ankles. A few years ago, I held a two day running workshop with legendary Irish marathon runner Catherina McKiernan who specialises in Chi Running. One of the things I've never forgotten were her words: "It's very difficult to injure a relaxed muscle". It is also, however, difficult to remember to stay relaxed for the entire duration of your run but it's worth paying attention to as much as you can.

Build up gradually

Gradual progression is built into the structure of the program itself, and you can always repeat runs as you need to. If you try to push your body too far beyond what it is capable of it will always push back. You probably won't get injured right away, but problems will start to store up for later on down the road.

You'll know if you're pushing too much or not taking long enough recovery between runs because your body will talk to you. Everyone's body has a voice but few of us are tuned in enough to know how to listen. The conversation is subtle but if you immerse yourself in the process of running you'll soon start to hear the noise.

You're in this for the long run (pun intended), so take your time to build it up, listen to the signals your body gives you and you'll avoid becoming an injured angry bear later on.

Body maintenance

Your body is a finely tuned system of systems, and it pays dividends to look after it.

Physical therapist

When I train for an event that requires me to step up the amount of running I do (still no more than three days in a week) I also step up the amount of maintenance work I do on my body. The easiest way to do this is to book a regular appointment with a physical therapist who specialises in running injuries.

Think of it as giving your body a regular MOT; tuning up your systems so they're at least aligned and ready to do their job correctly. Imagine a car with its wheels all bent out of alignment. It doesn't matter how good the engine is, that car won't be efficient and is likely to break down eventually. The same is true of your body. A therapist should at the very least be able to check your pelvis and spine are aligned which immediately reduces your injury potential.

Try to see a therapist every 6 weeks or so, though closer to once a month is better in my mind. And don't worry about the difference between physios, chiropractors and osteopaths. Just find someone who knows what they're talking about when it comes to running-related issues.

Massage

Sports massage is another great way to keep your body in check. I'm not talking about soft music and candles here; I'm talking about the Masters of Pain who will bring you close to tears. Sports massage is all about getting deep into the muscles and breaking down scar tissue before it has a chance to start causing too many problems.

A 30 minute massage on your legs once a month (or more frequently if you can afford it) will help flush out toxins and keep you feeling fresh. It also makes you feel like a pro runner, so enjoy every moment.

Warm up and cool down

Chapter 5 is devoted to the best ways to warm up and cool down properly, but I mention it here because it's another important part of the injury prevention mix.

Warming up

Aside from activating the glutes, stretching out the hip flexors, mobilising the spine and building in a 5 to 10 minute walk before your first little run, there's not much more you need to do to prepare for action.

Cooling down

At the end of the run there should be another period of walking for a few minutes to help flush out some of the lactic acid from the muscles and return your heart rate to something resembling normal. When you get in the door, a general stretching routine for the legs can help return your muscles to their original length. This won't necessarily prevent muscle stiffness the next day but it will at least stop them from gradually shortening over time.

Muscle soreness

It's really common, especially in the early days of the program, for your muscles to be sore the day after a run. This is completely normal, but it's important to learn the difference between muscle soreness and muscle pain. You may find that you need to walk down the stairs backwards for a day or two, or enlist the help of a friend to get off the loo. On the other hand you may get away with it and feel absolutely fine.

Either result is normal; if you don't feel sore after a run it doesn't mean you haven't worked hard enough or that there's something wrong. If you are following the program and making progress just consider yourself lucky you don't have to walk like John Wayne!

Common injuries

Although this book is not intended to be a diagnostics tool or rehabilitation aid for running injuries I want to cover a handful of injuries runners commonly get.

Foot pain

The structure in the foot that forms the arch on the instep is called the plantar fascia. Plantar fasciitis is where this area gets inflamed and it can become painful to walk on, let alone run. It is often caused by a tightness in the calf at the back of the lower leg, though this itself may have a root cause elsewhere in the body. Stretching the calf and rolling a rolling pin underneath the foot for a few minutes at a time can provide some relief. Your footwear selection could also be contributing to the pain so, if you haven't already done so, now is a good time to get yourself fitted with a proper pair of trainers (see Chapter 3).

Shin splints

The muscles along the front of the lower leg can become inflamed and painful when you run. It is nearly always down to your running style (especially if you land heavily on your heels) and a general weakness in this area. Try to run on grass as much as you can which reduces the impact. It can also be caused by building up too quickly, causing the muscles in the shin to grow quicker than the compartments that they are encased in, which can expand. This causes a pressure (compartment syndrome) and can be very painful.

If the pain doesn't go away after rest and a change of running terrain, shoes or both, it's time to see a physical therapist who can assess you more thoroughly.

Sore knees

This can come from a multitude of different causes. Commonly, it won't be anything to do with the knee, but rather an instability in either the ankle or the hip. There could be a tightness in one or more of the muscles in the thigh and weaknesses elsewhere. It really is best to get assessed by a specialist if you experience this and it doesn't get better (or if it gets worse) after a couple of weeks.

Hip pain

Pain around the hip area could also signify a number of different issues. Commonly, a weakness in the muscles in the outside of the hip can cause instability in the hip joint when you land on one leg as you run. To begin with, this is likely to cause no more than a feeling of mild awkwardness but, left unchecked, it can progress to hip pain or move further down the chain to the knees.

Simple hip stability exercises are a good starting point but if the problem persists it's off to the therapist you go.

Calf tightness

Another common area for tightness is the back of the lower leg. You may experience this during or after a run, perhaps the next day and it can be incredibly uncomfortable. It's nearly always related to either a pre-existing tightness or the way your feet are striking the ground as you run. Remember, forces through your body are increased when you run compared with walking so you may not have been aware of the tightness before starting to run.

If this happens, there are two things I would recommend you do before each run. The first is to stretch the calves by standing with your toes of one foot on a stair and dropping your heel down until you feel the stretch. If you then bend the knee you'll feel the stretch move further down the calf towards the ankle. Hold this for a few seconds in each position.

The second thing you could try is to roll a tennis or golf ball under the foot for about a minute. This will feel uncomfortable (it's a bit like foam rolling for the foot) but can help to release hidden tension in the plantar fascia that lies on the sole of the foot. I sprained an ankle doing one of those silly adventure races a few years ago (actually it was great fun but the idea of running through rivers and sand dunes sounds a bit whacky to most people!). Ever since then my ankle has been tight first thing in the morning. 60 seconds of ball rolling however, and it's good as new.

If tight calves and ankles are becoming a real problem then I'd recommend investing in a Trigger Point massage ball, which is like a wonky, slightly firmer tennis ball, but much better for the job. I've included a link to the Amazon page where you can get these from in the resources section.

Another cause of calf tightness can be your running style, which is covered off in Chapter 8. Pushing off too forcefully from your toes can cause more force than necessary to run through the calves so try to relax the ankles a little more as you run.

RICE treatment

If you get back from a run and are experiencing pain anywhere, it's your body's way of saying, "Look matey, something's not quite right here." Its immediate response will be to flood the area with fluids as it attempts to protect it from further damage. This inflammation is all very well and good, but it's usually a bit of an overreaction which can actually slow down the healing process.

As soon as possible, get some ice on the affected area (a bag of frozen peas is perfect as you can mould it to the shape of the muscle or joint). This will significantly reduce the inflammation, and when you remove the ice (after no more than 15 minutes) fresh, nutrient- and oxygen-rich blood floods the area and accelerates the healing process. Ideally you would cycle between ice and no ice every 15 minutes but, hey, you have a life to lead as well so just try to do as much as you can.

Once you have rested and iced the area, applying some compression will also help speed up recovery. You can get neoprene supports or just use a tight bandage on the area without actually cutting off your circulation! If the injury is in your leg you should also try to elevate it for a while. Lifting it above the level of your heart will prevent blood from pooling in the area and allow more of the fresh stuff to make its way down there (or up there, depending on your perspective).

So that's your RICE treatment for running injuries: Rest, Ice, Compress, Elevate. If you have a persistent injury no amount of words in a book will hold a candle to seeing a running injury specialist.

Compression clothing

I mentioned compression in the RICE section, but it deserves a heading of its own because it can also be an injury prevention strategy. There are entire companies dedicated to developing and marketing compressions gear for runners. The theory is that compression increases blood flow to the area, aids in venous return (getting the blood back to the heart) and reducing muscle vibration. The reality is that you're never going to be able to quantify the benefits of wearing compression clothing but in my experience I've found it to help with creating a more stable, 'better' feeling when I'm running. Compression socks are perhaps the most popular item and a good starting point, especially if you've suffered from calf issues.

Compression wear can also be used post-run to aid recovery. Many runners even admit to sleeping in the stuff which I can't help but find a bit weird but hey, each to their own. I have provided a link to some compressions clothing I use personally in the Resources section at the end.

Taping

The relative new kid on the block is physio tape. Whilst wrapping niggles up in a sticky plaster isn't a long term solution, the evidence is that using products such as KT Tape (my personal favourite) on tight areas can allow you to continue training safely and pain free whilst you work to resolve the problem.

The special tape is designed to increase blood flow to the applied area, and provide support whilst you exercise. Physios often recommend it as part of a rehabilitation protocol, but you can purchase and apply it yourself using various video guides to be found on the Internet.

Just remember that pain is your body's way of telling you something isn't right. Muscle soreness for a day or two after a run is one thing, but start tuning into your body and determining which signals are warning shots. Taping can help you continue to train, but always seek the help and advice of a physio if it's not helping. I have provided a link to KT Tape in the Resources section at the end (they also have a load of great videos on their website showing you how to apply it effectively).

Injuries and niggles are frustrating and at some point in your running career you may be sidelined. Take steps to reduce how often this happens and, if it does, just accept that you need to work through it and that you'll be back on your feet eventually.

Chapter 7 – What should I eat to fuel my running?

Just to be clear, this chapter isn't designed to be a nutrition program. Hopefully, though, it will serve as a guide to help you make some smarter decisions when it comes to the foods you choose to fuel your body with whilst on your running adventure.

Many beginners choose to take up running in an effort to lose weight. Ironically it's one of the least effective weight-loss strategies – certainly it's far from being the most time-efficient. Regardless, it makes sense that if you're embarking on a healthy lifestyle and running is a part of it you should be armed with at least a guide to 'runner food', which is what I aim to provide in this chapter.

Carbs

Perhaps the biggest myth in the running world is that we have to live with a pasta-loaded intravenous drip attached to our arm. Pasta, rice, potatoes, bread, porridge... these foods should form 100% of your diet otherwise you'll run out of energy and pass out mid-run.

This kind of hearsay 'advice' can lead to weight gain, low energy levels, nutrient deficiency and digestive issues. I'm not saying that you shouldn't eat any of these foods – most of them are pretty good in fact – I'm just saying that we shouldn't be eating them in the quantities that most of us do.

Pile your plate high with pasta to refuel after your 30 minute run and most of the sugars it contains will be sent right to your fat cells for storage. Starchy carbs are great energy-dense foods but the problem is that it's easy to eat more than is required (our muscles can only store a limited amount of the stuff). However, if you are going to eat them (and no doubt you will) stick with quinoa, sweet potato, rice, oats, potatoes and wheat-free pasta.

Wherever possible, try to eliminate gluten. Even if you're not gluten-intolerant this particular protein is likely to disagree with your digestive system, cause bloating and overload your liver. It's just not worth it when there are so many alternatives.

Load up on your nutrient-rich carbs like veggies, fruit, beans, pulses and legumes. Not only are they higher in the anti-oxidants your body needs to keep rebuilding and repairing after a workout, they contain more fibre and you can eat more of them.

Fats

If you've heard the one about runners needing shares in Hovis, you've probably heard the one about how we should stick to a low fat diet. More breaking news just in: you don't.

Fat is fine, in fact it is essential, just be careful where it comes from. The best sources are oily fish (salmon, sardines, tuna, mackerel, pilchards), coconut oil (exceptionally good for us), nuts and seeds (especially chia), olive oil, eggs (the yolks are full of healthy fats and nutrients) and avocados.

If you load up on these foods each day not only will you feel more energised and have fewer hunger pangs but you'll be providing your body with a flood of anti-inflammatory omega-3 oils that will rush around your system and deal with the inflammation that naturally occurs.

Incidentally a diet high in grains can cause chronic inflammation in your artery walls. The body's natural defence against inflammation is to lay down cholesterol (and you thought this was bad – it's actually your friend!), patching it up like a plaster.

Omega-3 fatty acids come along and sweep the inflammation aside so if you're not getting enough of them your grain-rich diet can end up being the source of high cholesterol and heart disease.

Poor old cholesterol gets such a bad rap when all it's trying to do is help!

One final labouring of the point, just in case you missed it: fat doesn't make you fat. That's the job of starchy carbohydrates and sugar, neither of which provide any significant levels of nutrients alongside their calorific punch.

Protein

Most runners – most people for that matter – struggle to get enough protein in their diet. Protein (meat, fish, poultry, eggs, dairy etc.) is made up of amino acids which we break down and use to repair and build every cell in our body.

Every cell. From those in your eyeballs, to the ones in your hamstrings. When you exercise you create teeny, tiny, microscopic tears in your muscles. This is the stress that causes the overload that helps you become stronger and make progress with your running.

When you rest between runs your body rebuilds these tiny tears using the amino acids from your protein-rich diet. If the building blocks aren't there, progress is a slow process!

Try to increase your protein intake at each meal. If you're dropping down the amount of starchy carbohydrate you're eating you can replace it with protein and veg. Nothing quite like a nice, big, fat juicy steak or salmon fillet accompanied by a mountain of green veg and a small portion of quinoa.

Apart from cake, maybe. Cake's pretty good too. But for a runner who wants to fuel an ever improving performance, let's go for the steak and veg.

Nutrients

Five-a-day? Pah! I laugh in the face of five-a-day. This was only really relevant back in the '60s when they were determining the levels of nutrients in a portion of fruit and veg. Back then our soil actually contained some nitrates but thanks to over-farming and routine use of chemical fertilisers and pesticides the nutrient quality of what ends up on our plates is far from what it was for previous generations.

Add to that the further degradation you get when you boil the life out of your poor veggies or, even worse, zap them in the microwave and you get an almost nutrient-devoid food. Worse, you *think* you're hitting your target which lulls you into a false sense of security, leading to impaired immune function and poor cellular health.

So what's the solution?

Number one: eat more veggies.

Number two: eat most of them raw or very lightly cooked.

Number three: aim for 10-a-day including fruit.

Number four: make smoothies and juices. Not only does this break down the starchy membranes of the veggie cells creating an almost instant hit of nutrients into your blood stream, but it's far easier to drink multiple fruit and veggies than it is to eat them.

Number five: don't discount supplements. A supplement should do just that – supplement your diet, not stand in place of it. Personally, I supplement with omega-3, vitamin D and magnesium, as well as taking a greens drink once a day. I also put away around 8-10 portions of the fresh stuff daily as well. This is your big lever – get pulling.

Water

It is absolutely crucial that you hydrate properly. If even the thought of upping your water intake to the recommended litre of water per 50lb body weight makes your pelvic floor start to twitch then you'll need to increase it gradually.

Try drinking an extra glass in the morning, sipping from a bottle through the day and then an extra glass in the evening. Increase it gradually and give your cells a chance to acclimatise to this new nicely-soaked environment and you'll reap the rewards as well as avoid the multiple trips to the loo.

If your cells are dehydrated it becomes very difficult for nutrients to pass across the membrane. This generally slows everything down: from your digestive system, to your fat metabolism, to your liver health. When you start to increase your activity levels by heading out for a jog a couple of times a week, your body is going to need to be properly hydrated more than ever. Tiredness, poor recovery, and muscle cramps can all frequently be traced back to dehydration.

A good way to check your hydration level is to take a look at the colour of your wee. Go ahead, take a look, I'll wait here.

What colour was it? If it was more golden syrup than pale straw it's probably time you took on some more water. Don't worry about taking water with you on your runs, unless it gives you an extra boost of confidence. From a physiology point of view there's no benefit to taking on water in a run lasting under an hour.

Anti-nutrients

Let's face it: you're learning to run, not training for the Olympics. You're going to have food and drink that doesn't line up 100% with your goal and that's fine. Life is about balance and I'm certainly not going to say that I never deviate. But it is a good idea to understand what some of the anti-nutrient foods do to us so our choices are informed.

Let's take a look at three of the most common ones.

1) Sugar

Put simply, you just don't need sugar in your diet. You'll get plenty from your fruit and veg without having to add in extra. You certainly don't need sports drinks to give you energy, despite what the marketers tell you. Try to limit the amount you consume and when you do eat or drink it take note of how it makes you feel immediately and in the hours after. When your insulin response kicks in it can often leave you feeling lethargic and craving more sugar.

2) Caffeine

A black Americano or espresso in the morning probably won't do you any harm. In fact, it may even be beneficial. Too much, though, and your cortisol levels will be off the chart. Add a load of cream and sugar to it and you start creating other problems. Try and limit caffeinated drinks to the morning when your cortisol levels are naturally high.

That way it's less likely to disrupt your sleep which, if you remember, is where you recover from your run and make your progress.

3) Alcohol

You can just about argue a cup of coffee into a performance-fuelling nutrition program but it's a bit more of a challenge with the booze. Believe me, I tried. I really did. But the fact is, the stuff is only ever going to put the kibosh on your progress. It'll overload your liver and too much in one sitting is likely to scupper your plans for a run the following day. I know that this news probably won't stop you from having a glass or two this weekend but, hey, I had to mention it.

Eating before you run

How you time your food before you run depends on how strong your stomach is. Some people can eat and then run within 30 minutes; others need to leave it at least a couple of hours.

You'll need to experiment to find the best way to time your food – start off with leaving it an hour after a light meal before heading out. The most common sign that you haven't left it long enough is a side stitch.

Morning runs

Try having a glass of water and a banana 30 minutes before heading out and then eating a fuller breakfast when you return.

Lunchtime runs

Have a mid-morning snack of some fruit and nuts, and then head out before returning for your lunch.

Evening runs

Have a mid-afternoon snack of some fruit and nuts or a smoothie, and then head out for a run after work before your dinner. Have your dinner when you get back.

Eating after you run

Post-run nutrition is another of those things that's hammered up in my opinion. You'll often hear that you need to eat within 30 minutes of finishing your run otherwise you'll start the next day with only half a tank of fuel.

Eating after your run isn't a bad thing to do, but often runners get so hung up on feeling like they *have* to get something down their necks that they grab the first thing that comes to hand. When you're tired from a run, that's not necessarily going to be something healthy.

If you're following the *Beginner's Luck* program you're not running every day so it's a fairly safe bet that your muscles will be fully stocked by the time you head out again two or three days later.

The final nail in the coffin for this piece of advice is that you're not even going to come close to depleting your stores. Just eat a balanced diet as outlined above, eat when you're hungry (rather than when you're bored / tired / emotional / someone puts a plate of biscuits in front of you), and don't worry too much about 'refuelling' after your run.

Power foods

Whether you're a runner or just someone who wants to look after yourself, here are 12 foods I would recommend you keep in your store cupboard or fridge.

1) Coconut oil
2) Eggs
3) Oats
4) Broccoli
5) Almonds and walnuts
6) Organic, grass-fed butter
7) Frozen berries
8) Almond butter
9) Raw cacao
10) Bananas
11) Spinach
12) Olive oil

Clearly there are other things you should have in store, but if you came to my house, 99% of the time you'd find all of these ingredients.

Simple Switches

You might consider making these simple switches to your nutrition, especially if you're trying to improve your energy levels or lose weight.

1) Cereals and milk >> porridge and chia

Wheat-based cereals like Weetabix and Shredded Wheat may have convincing marketing campaigns behind them but when it comes the starting your day you can easily do a lot better. Instead, switch to porridge made with oats and chia seeds, with added nuts, seeds and fresh fruit.

2) Sandwich >> Hard boiled eggs & quinoa salad

The sandwich is such a staple part of our diets that it can be hard to imagine an alternative that would match it for simplicity and convenience. But boiling a couple of eggs up the night before along with cooking up some quinoa means your morning routine takes no longer than normal. You then just need to sling together some other salad items, smother it in a nice oily and herby dressing and pack it all up in a Tupperware container along with a healthy dose of smugness.

3) Late evening chocolaty snack >> Clean Chocolate
Chocolate is actually pretty good for you as it's packed with healthy antioxidants. Unfortunately it's also pretty bitter which is why commercial chocolate is also packed with sugar. So try making your own clean chocolate, by melting 100g coconut oil and mixing it with 100g chopped nuts and 25g 100% cocoa powder. You can squeeze a little agave in there as well, before pouring it into a plastic container and leaving in the freezer to set for half an hour before turning out and chopping into chunks.

4) Chips >> Sweet potato wedges
These are really easy to make just by chopping sweet potatoes into wedges and baking in the oven for half an hour with plenty of coconut oil.

5) Soft drinks >> Water
Even the low cal soft drinks are really bad for you - there's no other way of putting it. Limit the number of toxins you put into your body, which the liver then has to work hard to process. Poor weight loss results and / or flagging energy levels can often be tracked back to too many toxins and sugar in the diet and soft drinks are a major contributor.

6) Tea and coffee >> Roobois and Tulsi
Like chocolate, coffee is another great source of antioxidants but when you add loads of milk and sugar or drink too much of it you negate the benefits. If you have trouble with sleep then you definitely want to look at better managing your caffeine intake. Switch to herbal teas, in particular Roobois (also known as red bush) and Tulsi teas. Both of these are naturally caffeine-free and taste great.

You don't *need* to make any changes to your diet in order to learn how to run. Eating well can certainly help your progress, but it's not essential for the *Beginner's Luck* program to be effective.

For some example recipes ideas visit the companion website: www.runningbygeorge.com/beginners/nutrition.

Chapter 8 – How can I improve the way I run?

If you have the ability to walk, chances are you have the ability to run. So off you go, putting one foot in front of the other. That's all there is to it. Just run. It's such a natural thing to do (or at least it *should* be), that we don't need to think about *how* we do it. Do we?

What about if we were going to learn how to play golf? Or tennis? What would we do then? Try and figure it out ourselves? Of course not – we'd get a coach or, at the very least, we'd read up on the correct technique. We'd take time to learn the skill; the movements, the balance, the shortcuts to efficiency. But running? Perhaps because it's natural it doesn't cross our minds that there's a technique and a skill to it.

A few years ago I did a triathlon. Now, I'm a reasonably fit guy but I tell you what, I suffered in that pool. Four lengths in and I was stopping to gasp a life-giving breath at the end of every other length. Thank goodness for the disguise of a hat and goggles so nobody could tell it was me as I huffed and puffed my way through all 16 lengths.

Before I got in the pool I had been watching other swimmers gliding their way effortlessly up and down the pool. I could tell that I was clearly much 'fitter' than some of them were but that didn't seem to matter. They still destroyed my swim times thanks to their superior efficiency.

I could swim, but they could SWIM. Why should you care about my disastrous triathlon efforts? Because the same thing happens to runners who don't pay attention to the way they run. And I'm not just talking about beginners either – I've taken dozens of workshops around the UK and Ireland helping experienced runners tweak and improve their technique. This stuff makes a difference. A difference in terms of your efficiency (and thus ease and enjoyment) but also your injury risk.

Right now, you can already run.

You can already put one foot in front of the other, but what if you're burning through your energy stores faster than you need to, making life harder than it needs to be? What if you could upgrade your style? What if I could give you four or five hacks that would make you glide across the earth more effortlessly? The good news is that you can improve your technique, and we're going to start with the most fundamental part of running form.

Breathing

If you're running for more than a couple of seconds you're breathing. I think we can both agree on that. But the question is *how* are you breathing? Although we all breathe, the most efficient runners breathe in a way that maximises the amount of oxygen they can draw into their lungs.

When I was 8 years old I lived in Berlin. My Dad used to take me out running on his lunch breaks around Charlottenburg and he taught me some valuable lessons in those early days. The first lesson he taught me was how to breathe. Most runners are unaware of the way they breathe. I know this to be true because I always ask the question: "Do you know how you breathe?" Nine times out of 10 the answer comes back as no.

If you are currently unaware of how you breathe when you try to run, it's time to get excited because this single sub-chapter could be the most important thing you ever read about running.

"Get rhythm,
When you get the blues,
Get rhythm,
When you lace up your running shoes..."

...sang Johnny Cash. Modified just ever so slightly.

And that's exactly what you have to do when you run. You need to integrate the rhythm of your feet into the rhythm of your breathing. Your feet striking the ground provide the beat that drives your breathing, and your breath provides the metronome that keeps you going.

This deeper, measured breath feeds your muscles with the life-giving, contraction-powering oxygen that they need. It gives you focus; it becomes the rhythm of your run.

When I talk about rhythm I'm talking about timing your in and out breaths with your feet landing on the ground. So, for example (and this is how I recommend breathing in most instances), as your right foot contacts the ground you breathe in for one. Then your left foot hits the ground and you breathe in for two. You take another step on your right and you breathe out for one, then your left, and you breathe out for two.

In – in – out – out.

Right, left, right, left.

What happens when you get the breathing right is that you a) take in more oxygen to feed the muscles, and b) hold the air in your lungs fractionally longer so that the carbon dioxide has a greater chance of diffusing back out of the blood and being expelled.

Because of these deeper, more oxygenating breaths, your heart doesn't have to beat quite so fast because there's more air available. It can get the same amount of oxygen to the working muscles for less effort. Do you think that's going to have an impact on how hard you find your running? Damn right it is!

This, combined with the Golden Key will transform your ability to run, so it is worth paying attention and learning how to do it. I have recorded a short video on the companion website describing this technique: www.runningbygeorge.com/beginners/breathing.

Posture

Do you like magic? I do. I've always been fascinated by it; I know that it's just an illusion but the effects are no less impressive. I want to show you a magic trick right now.

Stand up for a moment and reach into your pocket. Pull out the invisible piece of string that's in there (a bit of imagination is required here, especially if you don't even have pockets), and tie it to the crown of your head. Now pull yourself upwards to the ceiling with that piece of string, hold the position with your body, and let your arm hang back down by your side.

What do you notice? Should be a few things. Number one: you probably just 'magically' grew an inch or more. Number two: you just drew in your deep core stabilisers without having to think about it (that's the tightness in your tummy you're now feeling). A nice side effect of this is that if you have a few pounds to lose you probably look like you just dropped half a stone – now *that's* magic! Number three: you've just improved the alignment of your vertebrae.

All of these things are significant. When you run, this is what your posture should be like. For most runners the reality tells a different story: slouched shoulders, upper body angled towards the ground, spine contorted into all manner of uncomfortable positions. This is like me swimming in that triathlon – way more effort than necessary.

Lifting yourself tall makes a big difference but you'll need to work at it. You'll do it for 30 seconds and then forget. All of a sudden you'll be back to your old posture until something reminds you to take out that piece of string again. (You don't actually need to do the whole pocket / tying / arm in the air thing each time or you'll look a bit daft. Just use your imagination!)

Arms

Your arms contribute more to your running than you might imagine. Try to swing them front to back instead of side to side. They don't have to be arrow straight but neither do you want them to cross over the centre line of your body. If your shoulders tend to round forwards (often due to spending a lot of time sat down at a desk or in a car) your arm swing will more naturally cross this centre line. You'll need to work harder to 'open up' the chest and rotate your shoulders back.

It wants to feel natural rather than forced; otherwise you'll just create a whole new set of problems. Bend your elbow to around 90° and feel the arm drive to the rear rather than out in front of you. A slight stretch across the front of your shoulders as your loosely grasped fist pulls back to the level of your hip should create just enough tension to spring it forwards so your elbows come in line with the same point.

In the early stages of the program you can use the walk phases to shake out the arms and ensure that tension doesn't start to build up. As the program progresses you may need to do this shaking out on the run. I do this every few minutes – just let your arms dangle by your side for two or three steps before bringing them back up again.

Foot strike

The more you get into running the more you'll be exposed to other articles, video clips, and the opinions of fellow-runners. Nothing divides the running community quite like the subject of foot strike (apart from maybe running with or without music!).

It's a *fact* that we are designed to run on our mid- or forefoot. It's an *opinion* that this is how you should run. With a well-fitted pair of running shoes heel striking is going to be just as efficient and safe as hitting the ground with your forefoot. But none of that matters, as I'll show you in a second.

Firstly, though, just to drive the point home about how we're designed to run, try this little experiment. Take off your shoes and socks and run across the garden barefoot. I often wonder how many people will actually do this! I never carry out 'instructions' in a book but that doesn't really matter because I'm sure you can imagine how you would run if you did actually do it.

You would almost definitely NOT land on your heels. There's just way too much impact and beside, the body has developed an intricate spring system called 'the foot and ankle' which means you're far better off on the ball of your foot.

So why doesn't it matter how you 'think' you should run? Because if you start to think about it your muscles will lock up, your joints will become stiff and you'll forget to think about all the other technique points we just discussed.

Your foot will contact the ground and roll through the foot strike the way it is designed to if you hold good posture, lean forwards slightly from the ankle and relax. Don't even think about it. Don't think about pushing off with your toes (far too much tension in your calves) or lifting your toes up as you swing your leg through (far too much tension down the length of your shins). Just relax and instead think about lifting tall and leaning from the ankle.

You should try to run quietly, without your feet slapping down hard on the pavement so listen out for what's going on.

There is a video on the website explaining running technique in a little more detail if you'd like a more graphical explanation: www.runningbygeorge.com/beginners/technique

Practice

Running at this stage is about practice. The reason most beginner runners make such stellar progress in the early days (think about it – you'll make a 300% increase in the amount of running you do in the first two weeks of the program alone!) isn't because you suddenly become 300% fitter.

Sure, you'll make some gains in your muscle strength and aerobic fitness early on but the majority of your improvements will come from the adaptations your nervous system makes. In other words, you become a more skilful runner. Practise something enough times and eventually it becomes second nature: catching or hitting a ball, writing your name, riding a bike... it's all about practice. The same is true of running.

Every time you go out, think of your running as practice. You're getting better at the skill of running. That doesn't mean it has to be perfect every time you go out. We're not striving to achieve perfect technique; we just want it to be good enough so that it's not an issue. Good enough efficiency and minimised chance of injury. But by thinking about running as practice rather than just 'going for a run' or 'training', all of a sudden you have another marker for progress and another goal to achieve on each run.

Chapter 9 – How do I run faster?

The *Beginner's Luck* program is all about teaching you how to run continuously for 60 minutes and beyond. It's about confidence in your ability to keep putting one foot in front of the other, to create a habit of regular running and most of all how to enjoy it.

I've talked a great deal about how the Golden Key of learning to run this way is to keep your pace as slow as possible. The slower you go the longer you can run for without having to take a break, but at some point running a bit faster may become more important to you.

When running faster becomes important

Running faster may never be important to you. You may find that you're perfectly happy with just enjoying being able to get out there and running for half an hour or so, just enjoying the wind in your hair and the sense of freedom it gives you.

But one day you may decide that it'd be nice to just get a little bit quicker. If you get to the point where you do a race like a 5k or 10k all of a sudden you have a benchmark. You have a 'personal best', otherwise known as a PB.

It's amazing how much of a draw it becomes to try and then beat that time: to push yourself a little harder and a little faster, to see how much more you are capable of, to set new personal records. I must stress again, the objective of *Beginner's Luck* is to become confident with running so it's important not to start thinking about speed until you've reached this level.

Always remember that running faster is harder, and that to begin with you won't be able to keep the pace going for as long.

Why is running faster is harder?

Running faster requires your muscles to work harder. Your heart then has to pump harder to get more blood around your body, which is why your heart rate and breathing rate start to increase. After a certain point (your 'threshold') you begin to accumulate lactic acid in your muscles which prevents them from contracting properly and then you physically have to slow down. Usually accompanied by lots of swearing and promises never to try running again.

The good news is that your threshold is a trainable limit which means that, with a bit of practice, you can increase the gap before your collapse-in-a-heap point. As a general guide, until you can run comfortably for 30 minutes you should concentrate on building up your aerobic endurance. This means turning that Golden Key and going slow every time you head out the door.

Once you can run non-stop for 30 minutes, however, you may want to consider a few faster-running strategies. There are various training techniques we can use to help improve our comfortable running speed. We are going to look briefly at three of them: interval training, threshold training and hill training.

Interval training

If you've built up through the *Beginner's Luck* program you will have already experienced interval training. Any time you intersperse periods of running with periods of walking or slower running, you're doing interval training. When you can run continuously for at least 30 minutes interval training can help you improve your speed, if that is part of your goal.

Think back to the early days in the program where you were running for a minute or two and then stopping to walk. Go back and repeat some of those sessions from Bobcat Week, only this time run faster during the worky bits and slow right down or walk during the recoveries.

It might feel strange stopping and walking now you've got to a point where you don't have to, but the idea of this type of session is that you work hard for a short period of time. If you don't allow yourself to recover, your next interval won't be much faster than your normal 'slow' running pace. This type of session is NOT about distance. I always talk about going for time rather than distance but it's still hard to avoid making a note of how far you've covered. In an interval session distance really isn't a factor.

In the interval session, intensity is king.

I'm not going to tell you how fast you should be running, but needless to say it should feel like you have to work for it. Say you're running a minute interval. You should be counting down those last 15 seconds. But then, as if by some kind of miracle, after a minute or two of easy jogging or walking you're ready and raring to go again for the next one.

If you feel like you could keep that pace going for a lot longer, you've got another level of intensity inside you. It takes a bit of experimenting to figure out how you respond to different speeds so just run it, find it and feel it.

Threshold Training

Let me just say right now, I LOVE threshold training. Not because it's fun (it's not, it hurts); but because you get a real sense of progress and very quickly too.

Whenever you do anything physical, your body will be producing lactic acid. Even now, sitting down and reading these words you're producing the stuff but fortunately your body can get rid of it quickly enough so that it never bothers you. It probably keeps up just nicely when you're running slowly as well but, as you begin to run faster, the rate at which you're producing it starts to get closer to the rate at which you are able to get rid of it.

The point at which these two rates meet is called your threshold, and this is where you want to be aiming for on your threshold runs. By giving your body a sustained dose of lactic acid it's forced to adapt and become better at dealing with it.

Threshold intensity should feel like about 8 or 8.5 out of 10 on a 'Rate of Perceived Exertion', or RPE scale (read: pain-o-meter). 1 is easy, 10 is legs about to fall off. Even at 8.5 you should be able to spit out a few words at a time. If it goes above this you're pushing it too hard, so slow down until your RPE drops back in check.

If you want to inject a bit of threshold running, just give yourself one dose a week. Again, I'm assuming you can hit at least 30 minutes non-stop at a slow pace to even consider threshold running. If you can, here's how I'd recommend you go about introducing it.

Start with a five minute jog warm-up, then step up the pace A BIT for three minutes. After three minutes, drop back down again to a really slow jog. Try and keep running if you can but if you really have to stop you either pushed it too hard or are just not quite ready for the Threshold Monster yet.

Recover for two minutes at this slow pace and then ramp it back up again for another three minute block of threshold intensity. It can take a bit of experimenting to get this pace right, as it may feel okay to start with and then the intensity builds up quickly if you have pushed it too hard.

Aim for three rounds of three minutes, each with the same two minute break in between. If this feels okay, next week push up to four minutes for each block. And then five. And then six.

If you can get up to three eight minute blocks with two minutes of recovery, frankly you're probably ready for a more advanced program so go check out the i10 Project, the iHalf or even the iMarathon if your running bones have been really tickled (more information on each of these in the resources section).

Hill training

The mention of the word hills is enough to strike fear into the hearts of most beginner runners, but in reality the hills are your friends. They are there to give you an extra challenge that is going to allow you to take things up to the next level. Lots of different ways to tackle hill training, but the easiest way to introduce them is to run a series of intervals up and down them.

The session looks a bit like what we talked about earlier in the interval training section, only this time your work interval is running up a hill, and your recovery is jogging or walking back down again. The benefits include increased strength, better anaerobic fitness (you're going to be breathing out your bum doing this, trust me!) and an increased confidence. Never again will you worry about a little bit of a gradient on a run. You'll tackle it head on and embrace the challenge; and all because you've been doing your hill training.

So, typical session would look like this. Warm up with at least five minutes of easy jogging; then find a suitable hill of about 5-10% gradient. Obviously, the steeper your hill the tougher it's going to be; but you don't want it too shallow either or you won't reap the rewards.

Run hard up the hill for one minute, bearing in mind that after about 10 seconds the intensity is going to catch up with you. A full on sprint is probably going to lead to bailing out before your minute is up, so take the first one a bit steadier and see how you feel.

When your minute is up stop running. Make a mental note of where you've ended up so you have a marker for your next run. Turn around and start to walk or jog back down the hill. When you get to the bottom, up you go again and try to get back to the same marker as you did on your first run (or beyond). Don't worry if you don't quite make it, but it's just good to have something to aim for.

Four or five of these hill repeats will serve as a bit of an initiation test. You'll either love it or you'll hate it but, either way, you'll feel amazing later on in the day and you'll be on your way to becoming a faster runner because of it.

A final word

Running faster is exciting, but please don't forget the purpose of the *Beginner's Luck* program. Establish the habit of running; then bring it up to a point where you enjoy it and are able to do it continuously for a reasonable length of time.

Running faster may never be on your radar and this is fine. But if you do decide you'd like to get where you're going a little quicker, intervals, thresholds and hills are three direct routes to achieving what you want.

This chapter deals with the basics of running faster, though if you decide to really go for it then I'd recommend checking out the follow up program The Running Apprentice (www.therunningapprentice.com).

The Running Apprentice is designed to take you from beginner runner to just plain runner, and I introduce more detailed sessions for experimenting with training strategies such as threshold running, fartlek, hill training and intervals. Not only will you become a faster runner, you will also become more familiar with most of the techniques you'll find in more advanced training programs.

Chapter 10 – How do I prepare for my first race?

First of all, you may decide to never take part in an organised race. It's not the point of the program, though it does seem to be a natural progression for many beginner runners once they have built up enough confidence to take on the challenge of an organised race.

Distance vs time

You'll have noticed that the *Beginner's Luck* program is based upon time. Every run is to a set time rather than a distance and the reason I wrote it like this is to encourage you to build your confidence running for longer periods. I also encourage you to run as slowly as you can to enable you to complete the set time period.

Although you *can* measure the distance you cover on each run of the *Beginner's Luck* program, when distance becomes the focus (as in a race), your running speed will determine how long you will be running for.

So there are other factors to consider, and we're going to take a look at a few of them now.

Why race?

The race itself is the easy bit. The real challenge is in the training you need to do in the weeks and months leading up to it. It's a journey you go on, with the race at the end, but along the way you learn a lot about yourself as a runner and as a person.

You have to make sacrifices, you have to commit, you have to make changes to the way you live your life. Around 97% of people who start a marathon will finish it. I would estimate that only around 50% of those who start training for a marathon actually make it to the start line.

Do the training and get to the start line and you'll have no problem with the race, whether it's a 5k or a marathon. You may have started and stopped running yourself in the past. One of the major reasons runners give for quitting is that they lose motivation. Having a race in mind that you're training for gives you focus which, in turn, can boost motivation.

There's also an enormous sense of satisfaction and achievement in completing something you've had to work so hard and long for. This sense of achievement is an incredible draw for many people whether they've experienced it before or not.

When are you ready to race?

A lot depends on the distance you're planning on racing over (you will probably be ready for a 5k before a marathon!), but really, it comes down to your confidence.

The major purpose of the program is to get you to a point where you feel confident and comfortable being able to go out there and run for as long as you fancy, and to build running into your life.

Don't take on the pressure of a race before you feel ready. Your training program will be spread over two, three or even four months so there's plenty of time to continue to build your running fitness. The difference is that you don't normally get to extend each week of training over as many days as you like, as you do in *Beginner's Luck*.

If you start to fall behind or feel as though you're struggling with the pace at which the program builds up, the pressure can be enough to put you off running completely and we don't want that. Let's take a look at some of the most common race distances.

5k

This is an obvious starting point for racing as it's a really accessible distance but will still give you that sense of achievement when the medal is hung around your neck. The faster runners will finish this distance in around 17 minutes but the majority tend to cross the line in 20 to 40 minutes.

In the UK, Ireland and various other countries around the world there is an excellent organisation called Park Run, which organises 5k races most Saturdays. These are free to attend and although you don't get a medal at the end you'll get an official time and get to be a part of a really well organised and welcoming family of mixed ability runners. Check out www.parkrun.com for details of your local event.

If you can complete the *Beginner's Luck* program there's no doubt that you would be able to complete a 5k race, and run the whole way.

10k

This is a much bigger challenge, but still plentifully accessible to the large majority of runners. Many runners will finish under an hour, with the faster ones closer to 30 minutes, but lots of runners take up to 1 hour and 20 minutes. A run / walk approach with equal amounts of both would get you round in about 90 minutes, and this is usually the time of the slowest finishers.

If you can get to the point in the *Beginner's Luck* program where you are running for 45 minutes non-stop you could be ready to take on the 10k challenge. Even if you're running at just a little faster than walking pace you would still cover about 7k in this time, so with a walk / jog finish you would cross the line in around 75-80 minutes.

And that's with no extra training – if you followed a dedicated 10k program you would take even less time.

Half marathon

This is the first of the big challenges, and it's not for everyone. Once you've got your confidence up in *Beginner's Luck*, a 5k or 10k is really achievable. It's about the same amount of running that you've already done by the time you get to the end of the program, so not an inconceivable leap.

The half marathon requires another level of commitment to get through. Whilst you could potentially run a 5k or 10k off your *Beginner's Luck* training, this won't be enough to see you through a half marathon, and 12 or more additional weeks of training will almost certainly be required.

However, you have two important things in your favour. If you have completed the *Beginner's Luck* program you have already overcome much greater challenges than you will face in a half marathon program. Training for a half just requires more of what you have already learned how to do.

Secondly, take a look at some of the slower runners who finish half marathons, many of whom will walk most of the way. They set off knowing that it was going to hurt, knowing it was a huge challenge, and maybe *not* knowing if they'd even finish at all. But it didn't stop them from doing it. With the *Beginner's Luck* under your belt, and a bit of extra preparation a half marathon is within your grasp.

The majority of half marathon runners finish between 1:45 and 2:15, with some taking closer to 3 hours. A benchmark half marathon time would be anything under two hours. Under 1:30 is getting seriously fast and the winners are usually around the 65 minute mark.

Marathon

Many runners consider this the ultimate race distance. "If you haven't done a marathon, you're not a proper runner", some even say. I'd completely disagree with that statement because there's more to running than just going longer and longer but, that said, the marathon does hold an almost mythical appeal.

If the draw of the marathon is too much for you to resist, there are a few considerations you should make before you get stuck in. If you've built your running up from scratch using *Beginner's Luck*, the best advice is to 'serve an apprenticeship' before thinking about the marathon.

When I interviewed Irishman Gerry Duffy about his win at the UK Deca Ironman Challenge in 2011 (that's 10 Ironman triathlons – 2.4 mile swim, 112 mile bike then a marathon – over 10 consecutive days) he spoke about serving many apprenticeships along the way before he considered himself ready to even begin training for it. He started running just a few miles each week in his late 20s as a way to lose weight and regain control of his life – the 30 minute video interview is over on the companion website: www.runningbygeorge.com/beginners/gerryduffy.

It was Gerry's inspiration that lead me to create The Running Apprentice Course, and I would highly recommend you pass through it on your way to race distances such as the half and full marathon.

You should definitely complete a handful of 5k runs and at least one 10k before deciding if you're ready to tackle the marathon. You may even want to run a half marathon before committing to the full distance, though this is not always necessary.

Most runners take between four and five hours to complete the race. Anything under three hours is very good and the elites will be closer to two hours (almost unimaginable!). Many runners will still be on the course at the six hour mark.

What if you don't want to race?

If after you've considered everything the idea of taking part in an organised event holds no appeal to you, there are many other options to help you stay focused and motivated to run. Once you have reached the end of *Beginner's Luck* and can run for an hour, you may decide to try and increase your speed and Chapter 9 shows you how to do just that.

You may want to extend your runs and challenge yourself as to how long you can run non-stop for. Or you may simply want to get out there and run because you now just love running! Try different terrains – running across muddy fields is very different to running on the roads – or drive to somewhere really picturesque and run there.

I've seen plenty of beginner runners go from having zero interest in running to entering half and full marathons. As you go through *Beginner's Luck* you will change as a runner. Your confidence will grow and your mind-set will change.

You'll be a different person at the end compared to the start, so even if you have no intentions of doing a race when you're a Bobcat, by the time you're a Lion you may feel more than ready.

Chapter 11 – Frequently Asked Questions

Since the first edition of this book was published, I've been privileged to witness hundreds of complete beginners transition into confident, happy runners. Many have expressed how their journey from beginner to 'real runner' has literally changed their lives; how much fitter, more confident and in control they feel now they have conquered the challenge of running.

Along the way many questions have been asked in the little coaching group I set up on Facebook to support beginners (which you're welcome to join any time you like www.facebook.com/groups/beginnersluck), so I want to answer some of the most common ones here.

#1. "What happens if I miss a workout?"
The program is designed in such a way that this doesn't matter. You can take as long as you like to move through each of the levels, so just move onto the next run in the sequence when you next head out the door. Sometimes life gets in the way and you may not get out running for a couple of weeks. Just get back in the saddle the first chance you get, even if it means dropping back a couple of levels to something you are confident you will be able to do.

#2. "I keep failing a particular level, how do I get past it before I give up?"
Firstly, remember that the real goal of the program is to get out running regularly, so getting stuck on a level doesn't mean you're not achieving something. Secondly,

most people have found that when they slow their pace even more they are able to get through the level comfortably. It doesn't matter if you're running at walking pace, you're still running. Speed is just a matter of scale.

#3. "Is running on a treadmill as effective as outside?"
I'd always encourage you to run outside whenever you can, but if you feel more comfortable on a treadmill or if the weather and light outside make it impossible, then that's just what you have to do. You can still learn how to run on a machine, but bear in mind that when you transition to the roads it may take a few runs for it to feel comfortable. It's not uncommon to find it much harder when you transition from one to the other but this will soon pass.

#4. "How can I avoid getting a stitch?"
Several things are thought to cause a stitch, but unfortunately some of us are just more prone to them than others. Try varying the time you leave between eating and drinking and starting your run, and learning how to breathe from your diaphragm instead of your chest. I shot a video on this to help you understand what you can do to avoid this really annoying niggle: www.runningbygeorge.com/beginners/stitch

#5. Should I be taking any kind of supplements?
There are no specific supplements that you need to take just because you are running, but I always recommend a starting point for health as supplementing with vitamin D, magnesium and omega 3. Personally I also take a

greens drink as well, but none of these are essential for running.

#6. "Can I do my 3 runs a week on consecutive days?"
You *can* do them on consecutive days, but if there's any way you can avoid it I wouldn't. You would be better off running only on the first and third days, even though that would mean you would only get two runs in that week.

#7. "Can I exercise on the other days when I'm not running?"
Yes! You can do whatever other exercise you enjoy on your non-running days but be prepared to listen to your body and take an unscheduled break if you're feel that you're not recovering properly.

#8. "My legs are still aching from my run 2 days ago - should I still run?"
It's really common to wake up the next morning feeling absolutely fine, only to find you can barely walk the day after that. This is called the Delayed Onset of Muscle Soreness, or DOMS. If you really are still in pain then I'd recommend just doing the mobilisers and going for a brisk walk to try and loosen things off, then if you feel better break into a bit of a run. But pain is your body's way of telling you to back off, so listen to the boss.

#9. "I used to run a lot but have fallen out of the habit. Whereabouts in the program should I start?"
One thing that I was initially surprised about was the number of lapsed runners who started Beginner's Luck. But when you stop running for a while (years in some cases) you're bound to lose your fitness so it makes sense

to go back to basics and build back up again. The advice I give is to find a point in the program that you are absolutely confident that you can complete, and start from there. It's better to finish strongly rather than struggle through it.

#10. "Some of the early sessions are hard to remember - what's the best way to memorise these for each run?"

There's a lot of stopping and starting in the first few sessions so yes, quite a lot to try and remember on the run! One of the simplest ways to remember is to write it on a piece of paper or your hand so you can check back as you run. Many members of the group have found the GymBoss app (see Resources section) to be useful as this can be pre-programmed with the desired number of intervals. At the time of writing I am still trying to find the right partner to help me develop an app for the program!

#11. "I have had a baby recently, is it safe for me to start running?"

This is definitely one to consult with your mid-wife or health visitor about, but in general if there are no complications after 3 months you should be safe to begin running. Many new mums actually go out running *with* their baby in the buggy. If you think this could work for you, go for a 3 wheeler with large pneumatic tyres and a long handle that you can push with one hand. My sister trained for a marathon with her baby in a buggy so it can absolutely be done, though it's clearly going to make things a little more challenging than running without.

Chapter 12 – Final words

Learning how to run is an adventure. It's about more than just building up to being able to run for 60 minutes; the process itself is the goal. Many beginners following this program will have tried – and failed – in the past to learn how to run. Getting back on that horse and having another bash is to be commended.

Every time you return from another run, however you think it has gone, you have achieved something. There *is* no such thing as a bad run; some days will feel easier than others, but each run will be good.

How you feel about running right now is going to change over the next few weeks. As your confidence grows and you realise how much more you're capable of you'll inevitably reach for more. You'll be a different person. Right now don't be overwhelmed or intimidated by how much other people may seem to be doing. They haven't lived your life. The only person you can change is you, and the only person who can change you, is you.

Running will teach you that you can never know for certain what you can or cannot achieve. When you break through the limits you currently hold for how far or how fast you can run, you'll begin to question other limiting beliefs you may hold concerning other areas of your life.

Running can empower you and change your life.

The only run you regret is the one you didn't do

Chapter 13 – The program

Each week the program builds from the runs you completed in the previous week. There are some significant landmarks along the way and you should take a moment to congratulate yourself when you reach them especially if you are moving into unchartered territory.

You can download a printable copy of the program with space to tick off the sessions as you go, by entering your email address in the box on www.beginnersluckbook.com.

You may find it helpful to write down the details of the earlier sessions on a piece of paper you can then take with you on your run, or jot them on your hand. The intervals change more often in these early sessions as you build up your running fitness and need to take regular breaks. The Gymboss interval timer can be useful to help you time these intervals and you can either get the iPhone or Android app, or the Gymboss device itself. See the links in the resources section.

Bobcat Week (week 1)

This week is all about getting started. You just want to discover where you are with things; take stock and settle into the program. Remember you can repeat any or all of these sessions as frequently as you like – don't move on until you are confident you can complete all three.

Session 1 (7 minutes running, 21 minutes total time)

Warm up with 5 minutes of brisk walking and then jog for 1 minute. Drop back to a nice slow walk for 2 minutes before moving back into a jog again for another minute. Continue alternating between 1 minute jog, 2 minutes' walk until you have completed 7 intervals. Finish off with a 5 minute easy walk cool down.

Session 2 (10 minutes running, 23 minutes total time)

Warm up with 5 minutes of brisk walking and then jog for 1 minute. Walk for just 1 minute before moving back up into a jog again. This next recovery goes back to 2 minutes before you start to jog again for another minute. Your next recovery is 1 minute, then jog 1 minute, walk 1 minute, jog 1 minute, walk 2 minutes and so on, until you have completed 10 intervals of jogging in total. Finish off with a 5 minute easy walk cool down.

Session 3 (12 minutes running, 30 minutes total time)

Warm up with 5 minutes of brisk walking and then jog for 1 minute. Alternate between walking and jogging a minute for 3 intervals. At the end of your 3rd interval, give yourself an extra minute of walking recovery (2 minutes in total) before setting out for another jog. Repeat this sequence, so jog 1 minute, walk 1 minute, jog 1 minute, walk 1 minute, jog 1 minute, walk 2 minutes for a further 2 rounds. By the end of this session you will have jogged for 12 intervals. Finish off with a 5 minute easy walk cool down.

Wildcat Week (week 2)

This week you will be taking your runs up to 2 minutes from last week's 1, and increasing the overall length of time you spend on your feet. You are still building into the program and getting used to the feeling of being out there running.

Session 1 (18 minutes running, 32 minutes total time)

Warm up with 5 minutes of brisk walking and then jog for 90 seconds. Walk for 1 minute then jog again for another 90 seconds. Walk another minute, jog another 90 seconds and then increase your recovery to 2 minutes. Repeat this whole sequence again for another 3 rounds. By the end you will have completed 12 intervals of 90 seconds each. Finish off with a 5 minute easy walk cool down.

Session 2 (18 minutes running, 31 minutes total time)

Warm up with 5 minutes of brisk walking and then jog for 2 minutes. Walk for 90 seconds then repeat this sequence of 2 minutes jog, 90 seconds' walk for 3 more intervals (4 in total). Next, jog 90 seconds then walk 1 minute and repeat this interval 4 times in total. Finally, jog for just 1 minute followed by 1 minute of walking and repeat this sequence 4 times in total. Finish off with a 5 minute easy walk cool down.

Session 3 (20 minutes running, 36 minutes total time)

Warm up with 5 minutes of brisk walking and then jog for 2 minutes. Walk for 90 seconds then repeat this sequence of 2 minutes jog, 90 seconds' walk for 6 more intervals (7 in total). Next, jog for 90 seconds then walk for 90 seconds and repeat this sequence 4 times in total. Finish off with a 5 minute easy walk cool down.

Lynx Week (week 3)

The last of the 'transition' weeks, you are starting to build up to some real running here with Lynx3 seeing you complete 8 blocks of 3 minutes.

Session 1 (24 minutes running, 42 minutes total time)

Warm up with 5 minutes of brisk walking and then jog for 3 minutes. Walk for 90 seconds then jog for 2 minutes. Walk for 90 seconds then jog for 1 minute. Walk for 90 seconds before repeating this 3, 2, 1 sequence for 3 more rounds (4 in total). Finish off with a 5 minute easy walk cool down.

Session 2 (23 minutes running, 34 minutes total time)

Warm up with 5 minutes of brisk walking and then jog for 3 minutes. Walk for 90 seconds; then jog for 2 minutes. Walk for 90 seconds then repeat this sequence for 4 more rounds (5 in total). Finish off with a 5 minute easy walk cool down.

Session 3 (24 minutes running, 36 minutes total time)

Warm up with 5 minutes of brisk walking and then jog for 3 minutes. Walk for 90 seconds then jog for another 3 minutes of walking. Alternate between the two, for 8 intervals in total. Finish off with a 5 minute easy walk cool down.

Cougar Week (week 4)

You hit a major landmark this week as you progress to running for 10 minutes continuously. This is an important psychological point in the program and things stop appearing quite so scary once you're completed this week.

Session 1 (25 minutes running, 37 minutes total time)

Warm up with 5 minutes of brisk walking and then jog for 5 minutes. Walk for 3 minutes then repeat for a total of 5 intervals. Finish off with a 5 minute easy walk cool down.

Session 2 (25 minutes running, 33 minutes total time)

Warm up with 5 minutes of brisk walking and then jog for 5 minutes. Walk for 2 minutes then repeat for a total of 5 intervals. Finish off with a 5 minute easy walk cool down.

Session 3 (30 minutes running, 35 minutes total time)

Warm up with 5 minutes of brisk walking and then jog for 10 minutes. Walk for 90 seconds and then jog for 5 minutes. Walk another 90 seconds then jog another 5 minutes and continue to repeat the 5 minutes jog, 90 seconds' walk for 4 intervals in total. Finish off with a 5 minute easy walk cool down.

Puma Week (week 5)

The halfway point in the program, but remember you can extend any of these weeks as you need to. In Puma week you are going to step things up to another level, as you progress to running for 25 minutes continuously. That's a decent length of time to be able to run for so high five yourself when you complete it.

Session 1 (24 minutes running, 28 minutes total time)

Warm up with 5 minutes of brisk walking and then jog for 8 minutes. Walk for 2 minutes then jog another 8 minutes. Repeat this sequence for 3 intervals in total. Finish off with a 5 minute easy walk cool down.

Session 2 (30 minutes running, 32 minutes total time)

Warm up with 5 minutes of brisk walking and then jog for 15 minutes. Walk for 2 minutes; then jog for another 15 minutes. Finish off with a 5 minute easy walk cool down.

Session 3 (25 minutes running, 25 minutes total time)

Warm up with 5 minutes of brisk walking and then jog for 25 minutes. Finish off with a 5 minute easy walk cool down.

Cheetah Week (week 6)

Another big landmark as you hit 30 minutes in this week. You will notice that the 'time spent running' and 'total time' figures are getting closer and closer together now as your body needs fewer breaks to keep the running going.

Session 1 (30 minutes running, 33 minutes total time)

Warm up with 5 minutes of brisk walking and then jog for 25 minutes. Walk for 3 minutes then jog another 5 minutes. Finish off with a 5 minute easy walk cool down.

Session 2 (35 minutes running, 38 minutes total time)

Warm up with 5 minutes of brisk walking and then jog for 30 minutes. Walk for 3 minutes then jog another 5 minutes. Finish off with a 5 minute easy walk cool down.

Session 3 (40 minutes running, 43 minutes total time)

Warm up with 5 minutes of brisk walking and then jog for 30 minutes. Walk for 3 minutes then jog another 10 minutes. Finish off with a 5 minute easy walk cool down.

Jaguar Week (week 7)

A whopping 45 minutes of running in 2 of this week's sessions tells you things are moving nicely in the direction of that magic hour marker.

Session 1 (40 minutes running, 45 minutes total time)

Warm up with 5 minutes of brisk walking and then jog for 20 minutes. Walk for 5 minutes then jog another 20 minutes. Finish off with a 5 minute easy walk cool down.

Session 2 (45 minutes running, 50 minutes total time)

Warm up with 5 minutes of brisk walking and then jog for 30 minutes. Walk for 5 minutes then jog another 15 minutes. Finish off with a 5 minute easy walk cool down.

Session 3 *(45 minutes running, 50 minutes total time)*

Warm up with 5 minutes of brisk walking and then jog for 25 minutes. Walk for 5 minutes then jog another 20 minutes. Finish off with a 5 minute easy walk cool down.

Leopard Week (week 8)

The final major landmark before you reach 60 minutes, as you run for 45 minutes continuously. A tough week as things continue to build at a rate of knots from the previous week so be prepared to repeat sessions as often as you need to.

Session 1 (50 minutes running, 55 minutes total time)

Warm up with 5 minutes of brisk walking and then jog for 30 minutes. Walk for 5 minutes then jog another 20 minutes. Finish off with a 5 minute easy walk cool down.

Session 2 (50 minutes running, 55 minutes total time)

Warm up with 5 minutes of brisk walking and then jog for 40 minutes. Walk for 5 minutes then jog another 10 minutes. Finish off with a 5 minute easy walk cool down.

Session 3 (45 minutes running, 45 minutes total time)

Warm up with 5 minutes of brisk walking and then jog for 45 minutes. Finish off with a 5 minute easy walk cool down.

Tiger Week (week 9)

You'll accumulate 60 minutes of running in this week which should tell you how close you are to the finish. Major achievement: well done.

Session 1 (55 minutes running, 60 minutes total time)

Warm up with 5 minutes of brisk walking and then jog for 45 minutes. Walk for 5 minutes then jog another 10 minutes. Finish off with a 5 minute easy walk cool down.

Session 2 (60 minutes running, 65 minutes total time)

Warm up with 5 minutes of brisk walking and then jog for 30 minutes. Walk for 5 minutes then jog another 30 minutes. Finish off with a 5 minute easy walk cool down.

Session 3 (60 minutes running, 65 minutes total time)

Warm up with 5 minutes of brisk walking and then jog for 45 minutes. Walk for 5 minutes then jog another 15 minutes. Finish off with a 5 minute easy walk cool down.

Lion Week (week 10)

This is it – the moment you've been building up to! With 29 runs under your belt by the time you get to the final run in Lion Week, running for an hour will seem like a stroll in the park. Enjoy the experience and don't forget to tell yourself how amazing you are for getting here.

Session 1 (60 minutes running, 65 minutes total time)

Warm up with 5 minutes of brisk walking and then jog for 50 minutes. Walk for 10 minutes then jog another 10 minutes. Finish off with a 5 minute easy walk cool down.

Session 2 (65 minutes running, 70 minutes total time)

Warm up with 5 minutes of brisk walking and then jog for 50 minutes. Walk for 5 minutes then jog another 15 minutes. Finish off with a 5 minute easy walk cool down.

Session 3 (60 minutes running, 60 minutes total time)

Warm up with 5 minutes of brisk walking and then jog for 60 minutes. Yay! You made it! Finish off with a 5 minute easy walk cool down.

Don't forget to download your printable version of the program over at companion website: www.beginnersluckbook.com.

Level	Session One	Session Two	Session Three
Bobcat Week	Jog 1min, walk 2mins, 7 times in total	5x (Jog 1min, walk 1min, jog 1min then walk 2mins)	4x (Jog 1min, walk 1min, jog 1min, walk 1min, jog 1min, walk 2mins)
Wildcat Week	4x (Jog 90s, walk 1min, jog 90s, walk 1min, jog 90s, walk 2mins)	4x (Jog 2mins, walk 90s). Then 4x (Jog 90s, walk 1min). Then 4x (Jog 1min, walk 1min)	7x (Jog 2mins, walk 90s). Then 4x (jog 90s, walk 90s)
Lynx Week	4x (Jog 3mins, walk 90s, jog 2mins, walk 90s, jog 1min, walk 90s)	5x (Jog 3mins, walk 90s, jog 2mins, walk 90s)	8x (Jog 3mins, walk 90s)
Cougar Week	5x (Jog 5mins, walk 3mins)	5x (Jog 5mins, walk 2mins)	**Jog 10mins**, walk 90s, then 4x (jog 5mins, walk 3mins)
Puma Week	3x (Jog 8mins, walk 2mins)	Jog 15mins, walk 2mins, jog 15mins	Jog 25mins without walking

Level	Session One	Session Two	Session Three
Cheetah Week	Jog 25mins, walk 3mins, jog 5mins	**Jog 30mins**, walk 3mins, jog 5mins	Jog 30mins, walk 3mins, jog 10mins
Jaguar Week	Jog 20mins, walk 5mins, jog 20mins	Jog 30mins, walk 5mins, jog 15mins	Jog 25mins, walk 5mins, jog 20mins
Leopard Week	Jog 30mins, walk 5mins, jog 20mins	Jog 40mins, walk 5mins, jog 10mins	**Jog 45mins** without walking
Tiger Week	Jog 45mins, walk 5mins, jog 10mins	Jog 30mins, walk 5mins, jog 30mins	Jog 45mins, walk 5mins, jog 15mins
Lion Week	Jog 50mins, walk 10mins, jog 10mins	Jog 50mins, walk 5mins, jog 15mins	Jog **60mins** without walking

Resources

There are certain resources I refer to throughout the book and here is where you can find them. Amazon is a great place to acquire most items you're ever going to need in this life, and running equipment is no exception.

Visit **www.runningbygeorge.com/beginners** for a list of all the direct links to the individual resources (correct at time of print).

Other training programs

As well as this book, I have a range of other programs that may, one day, be of interest to you.

The Running Apprentice
www.therunningapprentice.com

An 8 week course that leads you through some of the most common training systems you are likely to encounter in a 'proper' training program. The course is designed to bridge the gap between beginner runner and just plain runner.

i10 Project
www.i10project.com

10 week, 10k training program. As a pre-requisite you need to be able to run for at least 45 minutes non-stop before starting the i10 Project. The aim is to get faster with 3 targeted training sessions a week, and then complete a 10k race at the end of the 10 week program.

Intelligent Half Marathon
www.intelligenthalfmarathon.com

12 week, half marathon training program. Based on three runs a week plus a body conditioning program, information on nutrition, and personal support from Coach George and all the other runners on the same program.

Intelligent Marathon
www.intelligentmarathon.com
16 week, full marathon training program. Based on three runs a week plus a body conditioning program, information on nutrition, and personal support from Coach George and all the other runners on the same program.

Support material

I mention several supporting videos and downloads that are available for you on the companion website. Here is a list of them for your reference.

Hip flexor stretch
www.runningbygeorge.com/beginners/hipflexor

How To Breathe
www.runningbygeorge.com/beginners/breathing

Example recipes
www.runningbygeorge.com/beginners/nutrition

3D mobilisers for the spine
www.runningbygeorge.com/beginners/mobilisers

Glute activation
www.runningbygeorge.com/beginners/glutes

Breathing technique
www.runningbygeorge.com/beginners/running-technique

Dealing with a stitch
www.runningbygeorge.com/beginners/stitch/

Foam Rolling
www.runningbygeorge.com/beginners/foamroller

Recommended Reading

The Chimp Paradox - Dr Steve Peters

Start With Why - Simon Sinek

Tick, Tock, Ten - Gerry Duffy

Who Dares Runs - Gerry Duffy

Running With The Kenyans - Adharanand Finn

Born To Run - Christopher McDougall

There are also several running magazines you can pick up from most newsagents. Don't be put off by the impossibly fit looking runners on the front covers, they nearly always have plenty of useful information for beginner runners.

Once you've read a few of these magazines you'll realise that they tend to recycle the same ideas from slightly different angles, but that's not to say you won't continue to learn. Often two articles within the same magazine will contradict themselves but you're not reading them for the gospel of running (you already own that particular piece of work ;). The magazine and books I mentioned above can be quite motivating, and for a couple of quid a month that makes them pretty good value.

Printed in Poland
by Amazon Fulfillment
Poland Sp. z o.o., Wrocław